Prayer-
the Christian's Vital Breath

L. A. T. VAN DOOREN

PRAYER —
THE
CHRISTIAN'S
VITAL BREATH

L. A. T. VAN DOOREN

THE LATIMER PUBLISHING CO.
CARNFORTH, LANCS., ENGLAND

OTHER TITLES

By

L. A. T. VAN DOOREN

Prayer — the Christian's Vital Breath

L. A. T. VAN DOOREN

THE LATIMER PUBLISHING CO.

Carnforth, Lancs LA6 1AG, England

ISBN 0 946269 07 6

First Edition	..	..	1962
Second Edition	..	..	1963
Third Edition	..	..	1971
Fourth Edition	..	..	1974
Fifth Edition	..	..	1977
Sixth Edition	..	..	1978
Seventh Edition	..	..	1984

Photoset and printed in Great Britain by
Stanley L. Hunt (Printers) Ltd, Midland Road, Rushden, Northants

FOREWORD

by

DR. STEPHEN F. OLFORD

I WELCOME the opportunity to write a Foreword to Mr. Van Dooren's little book on prayer. It is not without significance that prayer is so often associated with the mountain top: Abraham worshipped God on Mount Moriah (Genesis 22: 5), Moses went up to commune with the Holy One of Israel on Mount Sinai (Exodus 19: 3); Joshua built an altar unto the Lord in Mount Ebal (Joshua 8: 30); Elijah prayed for fire and for rain on Mount Carmel (1 Kings 18: 36-37; James 5: 17); and so we could go on until we come to the blessed Master Himself, Who ever sought the solitude of the mountain top for meeting with His Father. How beautifully Matthew puts it, when he records that when Jesus had sent the multitude away, "he went up into a mountain apart to pray" (14: 23).

The mountain top is the place of perfect stillness, clear vision and pure air. Indeed, it is the place where the Christian breathes the rarified atmosphere of heaven. Whatever it costs, the Christian must climb these mountains of discipline and determination, if he is to know fellowship with God and reach the heights of a prevailing prayer life. Prayer is indeed the Christian's vital breath; but no Christian breathes truly or purely unless he has scaled the peaks of holy intercession.

Mr. Van Dooren's book has been written with the express purpose of pointing out the way to some of these peaks in the life of prayer. Young people, students, and older folk, will find these pages both profitable and pleasurable, not to say challenging.

3

As E. M. Bounds has so rightly said: "What the Church needs today is not more machinery, or better, not more organisations or more and novel methods, but men whom the Holy Ghost can use—men of prayer, men mighty in prayer. The Holy Ghost does not flow through methods but through men. He does not come on machinery, but on men. He does not anoint plans, but men—men of prayer."

It is my earnest hope that those who read these chapters will become men and women of the mountain top, men and women filled with the Holy Spirit—yes, men and women of prevailing prayer.

STEPHEN F. OLFORD,

CONTENTS

PRAYER—
THE CHRISTIAN'S VITAL BREATH

IS PRAYER NECESSARY ?

"Men ought always to pray . . ." *"Pray without ceasing . . ."*
"Continue in prayer."
"I will pray for you . . ." *"We must pray about the matter . . ."*
"The great need is for more prayer . . ."

THE clear statements of scripture, coupled with the words found so often on the lips of Christians, all emphasize the need and importance of prayer in the life of the Christian.

An informal discussion had taken place in a home on certain aspects of Christian work, concerning which the need for prayer had been stressed. Prayer had formed one of the main topics of the conversation. The young son of the householder had been a silent listener as first he had played with his toys and then later looked at his picture book. After the visitors had gone and he was having his nightcap, he suddenly looked up into his mother's face and said, "Mummy, if everybody should pray, why don't we pray more?". It was a telling question.

If the question were to be put to you concerning the need for prayer, in all probability you too would answer most emphatically, "Yes, every Christian should pray". If true prayer is so vital to the individual believer as well as to the Church of Jesus Christ, why then is there so little effective prayer? One answer is that prayer is dangerous to the powers of spiritual darkness and this reason in itself may be an explanation as to why the adversary uses all his strategy to prevent Christians from praying as they should. It is said,

"The devil trembles when he sees
The weakest saint upon his knees"

If it were possible to learn some technique, some cut and dried formula on a 'do it yourself basis', no doubt many would avail themselves of such an easy road to an effective prayer life. It is true we may learn from the Word of God and from the examples recorded therein. These reveal the prayer life of men of God. We may also learn from the advice and experience of mature Christians, but it is important that all should learn this simple and essential truth. *Praying is learnt by praying.* As you pray, so you learn to pray. As in many other aspects of the Christian life, the school of experience is where true prayer may be learnt and exercised.

It is significant that there is no record of the Lord teaching His disciples how to preach, but He took time to teach them how to pray and how not to pray. He spake parables on prayer—and yet in the hour of greatest need immediately prior to the Lord's betrayal in the garden of Gethsemane, the men who had heard most from the lips of the Lord concerning the necessity of prayer, were to be found sleeping. But a few moments before, the Lord had said to His disciples, "Pray . . ." He then withdrew Himself and kneeling down prayed to His Father, "and when He rose up from prayer, and was come to His disciples, He found them sleeping for sorrow". Sleeping—so soon! "And said unto them, Why sleep ye? rise and pray, lest ye enter into temptation" (Luke 22: 40-46).

Whilst staying in Moslem lands I have often been aroused at the first streaks of dawn by the call to prayer from the mosque. In the stillness of the early morn, it can be a piercing cry commanding attention. After the first pronouncements, that Allah is one God and Mohammed is his prophet, the call goes on to say "It is better to pray than to sleep." I have frequently thought of that cry—with its challenging demands as the light of day is breaking. I have sometimes thought it would be good if it could be implemented in a Christian context and brought home to the hearts of believers throughout the world.

You may be instructed and helped from the experience and writings of others. The Spirit of God will certainly use the Word of God to lead you to a new and deeper understanding of all that is meant by prayer, but finally, you will learn to pray as you pray, and as you pray, so you will come to know the meaning of true prayer.

Therefore, "Pray without ceasing . . ." "Continue in prayer . . ." Let this become the habit of your life, "For men ought always to pray and not to faint".

II

THE TRUE PURPOSE OF PRAYER

THE question might well be asked, "Why should Christians pray?" "What is the real purpose of prayer?" A little boy was asked why and when did he pray and his answer was brief and to the point: "I pray when I want something and when I do not think there is any other way of getting it".

Is that why you pray? Is that the purpose of your prayer?

To judge from many, it would seem to be that prayer has been so trimmed and narrowed down that it would almost fit into the neat formula of the little boy. No doubt the lad could be excused, having such a limited idea about prayer. At any rate, he was honest. But can you, as a child of God, be excused for having such a shrivelled and poor view of prayer? If you are honest, it may be that this is an apt summary of your prayer life in the past. You pray when you want something and cannot get it any other way. Did God intend that prayer should be an 'open sesame' or at the best, to be used when suddenly confronted with a special need? Is prayer intended to be an easy and handy form of escapism?

Is prayer meant to be nothing more than a convenient 'pipe line of supply' from heaven to earth? Is prayer intended to be one track only? What are your answers to these questions? Surely prayer is intended to be two track: two track in the sense that it is not only from earth to heaven, from the human heart to the source of supply, but also to be from the heart of God in heaven to the child of God upon earth, a revealing of the mind and ways of the Lord to His disciples here below.

What then is one of the principal purposes of true prayer? Prayer has been likened to a boat hook. As you stand in a little rowing boat and cast the hook on a line on to the nearby pier or jetty and then pull on the line, what happens? Slowly but surely the pier or jetty begins to move and to come alongside the small rowing boat! Does it? No, no, but as you pull on the line, the little boat slowly moves until it is alongside the pier or jetty. So it should be with prayer. By prayer it is not intended that we should try to bring God down to our level and to make Him bend, as it were, His will to fit in with what we desire and want, but rather is prayer intended to bring us into closer fellowship with God and thus more and more into line with His will and purposes.

It is God's intention that as we pray we should come to know more of His will and also be brought into the position where we desire that His will be done. Frequently it will bring us to that point at which He can begin to use us to the fulfilling of the very prayer that we offer.

Turn to the latter part of Matthew, chapter 9, where this principle is illustrated. In 9: 36 the need is stated—"But when He saw the multitudes, He was moved with compassion on them, because they fainted, and were scattered abroad, as sheep having no shepherd."

In verses 37 and 38, the Lord makes it clear as to how the need is to be met—"Then saith He unto His disciples, The harvest truly is plenteous, but the labourers are few; Pray ye therefore the Lord of the harvest, that He will send forth labourers into His harvest." There is a tremendous need, there is a harvest waiting to be gathered, but labourers are few. The need is to be met and the harvest is to be gathered, as believers pray that the Lord will send forth, that is, irresistibly thrust forth, those of His choice to accomplish His will. In this way, the Lord of the harvest first of all brings into active co-operation, by prayer those whom later He would use. Let it be re-stated, the need is so great that only the Lord of the harvest can meet the need. The harvest waiting to be gathered is plenteous, that is, is ripe and ready for gathering, but only those of God's choice can be truly used in this work. The need is for spirit-filled men and women and young people to go forth because the Lord thrusts them forth. But observe this as you proceed to read on into Matthew, chapter 10. You discover that the very ones whom the Lord has called into co-operation with Himself, firstly by prayer, are then sent forth to become in some measure the answer to their prayer.

This is how God frequently works. As you pray, so you come to know the will of the Lord in certain details. This begins to find expression in your praying, thus you are brought closer and more truly into fellowship with the Lord until you are in the position and ready for God to thrust you forth to work through you as He will, that is, to bring to pass His will that has been translated into your prayer. So it is that many a young person has learned of a particular need and as they have prayed, so the Lord has been able to move them towards the meeting of that need. Their pocket has been touched, or in some other way they have sought to advance the work in some part of the far-off mission field. Step by step God has been dealing with them and they have come into closer fellowship with their Lord, until finally, constrained by the love of Christ, they can do no other but say, 'Lord, here am I, send me'. Thus, they have gone—the answer to their own prayers!

Nehemiah of the Old Testament is an outstanding instance of a man of prayer. Turn to Nehemiah, chapter 1, verse 4, and you read "And it came to pass, when I heard these words, that I sat down and wept, and mourned certain days, and fasted, and prayed before the God of heaven".

The following verses deserve study as the heart of this man is laid bare, and he prays. Read on until you come towards the close of verse 11, where you discover that the man who has wept and fasted and prayed and confessed the sin of his people, and has called upon God to fulfil His promise, now places himself at the disposal of the Lord. He seeks to be ready should the Lord desire to use him to bring to pass God's own purposes for His people. The willingness to be used and the desire to be used finds definite expression in the next chapter. "Then the king said unto me, For what dost thou make request? So I prayed to the God of heaven. And I said unto the king, If it please the king, and if thy servant have found favour in thy sight, that thou wouldest send me unto Judah, unto the city of my fathers' sepulchres, that I may build it" (Nehemiah 2, 4 and 5).

'I prayed to the God of heaven . . . I said to the king . . . send me . . . that I may build.' The man of prayer went forth as the man of action to do, "what my God had put in my heart to do at Jerusalem" (Nehemiah 2: 12).

Prayer is not intended to be a quick and easy 'give me'. Prayer is an attitude of life, it is fellowship with the Lord and Saviour, a spiritual exercise, intended to be as much a part of the Christian life as breathing is to the physical life.

> *"Prayer is the Christian's vital breath,*
> *The Christian's native air . . ."*

III

CHOOSE THE PLACE
AND KEEP THE APPOINTMENT

WE all recognize the need for prayer, for more prayer—and yet more prayer. Nevertheless, so often the confession has to be made that prayer seems almost ineffective, is hurriedly skipped over, if not forgotten and omitted altogether.

'But,' says one, 'I really mean to pray, but the day speeds by and somehow there seems to have been little or no opportunity for prayer.' Days have a habit of becoming weeks, which very soon run into months, and, alas, lead on into years—years of prayerlessness. Another says, 'When I pray I find that many pressing duties come to mind, the things that I have forgotten and left undone.' Whilst yet a third person says, 'My main difficulty is that when I pray I very soon begin to go wool-gathering. My thoughts wander so that I seem finally to be almost frustrated instead of helped.'

How can these difficulties be dealt with?

Read Matthew 6: 6—"But thou, when thou prayest, enter into thy closet, and when thou hast shut thy door, pray to thy Father which is in secret; and thy Father which seeth in secret shall reward thee openly". What does it say? When you pray, go into your own room. Go into a room by yourself and close the door! Quite simply it means have a place where you can be alone with God, where in a very real sense you can shut the door upon the other calls and duties of this life and be quietly but definitely in the secret place with your heavenly Father.

Now turn to Mark 1: 35—"And in the morning, rising up a great while before day, he went out, and departed into a solitary place, and there prayed". The Lord Jesus rose early

14

to go out to a lonely spot, a place where He knew He could be alone with His Father, and there prayed.

These two scriptures should be underlined in your Bible. There is much that we can learn from them, but the point we desire to make now is that the Lord Jesus, both by precept and example taught that there should be a *place* for prayer and also a *time* for prayer. Failure to obey the teaching, failure to follow the example of the Lord, will frequently lead you into the difficulties stated at the commencement of this chapter, namely, wandering thoughts in time of prayer, if not complete forgetfulness, leading to a life of prayerlessness.

Think of one character from the Old Testament, namely Daniel, a man who uncompromisingly took his stand for God. He did so amidst circumstances which were not conducive either to godly living or open testimony, yet he was a man of true spiritual wisdom, a man whose life was characterized by true holiness. With Noah and Job he is singled out by the Lord as being a man of righteous living (Ezekiel 14: 14-20). Read in Daniel, chapter 6, and you will discover that Daniel was also a man of prayer. He had a *place* and *time* for prayer—"And Daniel's windows being open in his room toward Jerusalem, he kneeled upon his knees three times a day, and prayed, and gave thanks before his God, as he did aforetime" (Daniel 6: 10). Was this the secret of his godly living? Was this the secret of his uncompromising testimony to the Lord? Was this the secret of his courageous witness and his true spiritual insight? In the Book of Daniel there are other references to his prayer life, and to him came the voice from heaven, "O Daniel, a man greatly beloved . . . O man greatly beloved, fear not, peace be unto thee, be strong, yea be strong". Daniel was a man who had a *place* and *time* for prayer. Have you a *place* and *time* for prayer?

Why did the Lord Jesus teach and do as we have read in the Scriptures from Matthew and Mark? As you read the earlier verses in Matthew, chapter 6, so you will discover that the call to be alone with God in prayer is preceded by these words, "When thou prayest, thou shalt not be as the hypocrites . . .". The Lord is referring to a certain type of Pharisee who loved to stand in the open at street corners, or in the synagogue where they could be seen by everyone. This would at once mark them out, so they thought, as men of outstanding piety. Everybody would know that they prayed! They prayed so that they could be seen by men. Incidentally, the Lord says *that*, namely to be seen by men, was their reward—and the only reward that they would receive for such praying. What does it mean to be a hypocrite? The simple meaning of the word is to be a 'play actor', that is, one who plays or acts a part which is not true to his life. The Lord knew the human heart through and through. He knows yours and He knows mine. He knows how easy it is to give way to the desire to be seen of men, to be highly esteemed by others, to be thought well of, even if we know in our heart of hearts that we are not all that we appear to be. But, to be alone in a secret place with God in prayer is to be stripped of all play-acting—you are in the presence of your heavenly Father. You are not called upon to put on a good appearance before others, there is no demand to show off in any way whatsoever. You are alone with God.

Face this issue squarely. Be honest, sincere and unassuming in your praying. It is necessary that you should find somewhere which is equivalent to your room, with the door closed. For some, it will be possible to go into their own bedroom, others will have to think and look around for some other place. Remember, the Lord Jesus, when He wished to be alone with His Father had to go into a lonely spot on the hillside, or even on the mountainside. He had no bedroom of His own. Often when He slept out at night, possibly in some cave on the Mount of Olives, or in the open, He would be in company with His disciples. Therefore, in the darkness of the early morning He would rise and go to the secret place to be alone with His heavenly Father.

From the scripture in the first chapter of Mark, we find the additional emphasis on a *time*. There was never a man who was so busy as the Lord Jesus in His public ministry. Twice over in this same Gospel of Mark, it is recorded He had no time so much as to eat. Whenever He was near the centres of population He was thronged by the needy multitude. Others came for private interviews at night. Often during the day there were long and exhausting journeys to be accomplished on foot. The Lord was a man of almost ceaseless activity, but as a man of prayer, He rose early in the morning. He had a place and also a time for prayer.

As surely as you need a place, so also you need a time which must be zealously guarded so that the habit of prayer is formed right from the commencement of your Christian experience. Turn to Colossians 4: 2—"Continue in prayer, and watch in the same with thanksgiving;" This has been variously rendered, but always with the same emphasis. Persevere in prayer! Form and maintain the habit of prayer! Be steadfast and unwearied in praying! The habit of prayer is best formed and maintained as you have a regular time at which you keep an appointment with God. At first, habits do not always seem to be easily formed, especially as related to prayer, for it is ever necessary to bear in mind that there is an adversary who will do his utmost to interfere with the time-table! Nevertheless, as you quite simply yet definitely keep the appointment with the Lord, so you will discover that the habit thus formed will become a joy and a delight, not irksome in any way, but that part of the day to which you will look forward and anticipate continually.

Quite obviously, one of the best times of the day is first thing in the morning. Not many can break away from the legitimate and often pressing duties of the day. Furthermore, as one awakes refreshed by a night's sleep, it is surely fitting as well as desirable that in the freshness of the early morning, there should be conversation with the Lord.

Choose the Place. Observe the Time. **Keep the Appointment with God.**

Arising out of the consideration of these two factors, it will readily be seen that prayer becomes a regular part of the believer's life. It will not be crowded out. There is place and time for it. Furthermore, a very decided step will have been taken to the overcoming of the difficulty of 'wool-gathering' or wandering thoughts. You are alone with God. That will probably be true physically, but also by your act of will other things will be shut out and kept from interfering unduly with your time of prayer. By reason of the fact that you have come to the place and have set aside the time for prayer, you will in that way discipline yourself in some measure so as to concentrate your attention and thought during the time of prayer. Thus, without undue distraction from without and overcoming distraction from within, thoughts can be mastered and marshalled. Furthermore, as a child of God, you are indwelt by the Spirit of the Lord, and He will have the opportunity of directing your thought and leading you in prayer with the Lord. Of this aspect of the Holy Spirit's ministry we shall have more to say later. If your time of prayer is at a time when you are renewed in mind and body by the sleep of the night, and in that sense are fresh, then you will be much better fitted to engage in prayer-conversation with the Lord. You will be alert. This thought is also brought out in the scripture already referred to in Colossians 4: 2 where not only is the habit of prayer stressed, but clearly stated is the need to be alert, unwearied, praying diligently, with mind awake and responsive to the leading of the Holy Spirit. Thus this way you will be delivered from vain repetition, to which the Lord referred in Matthew 6: 7— "But when ye pray, use not vain repetitions, as the heathen do: for they think that they shall be heard for their much speaking".

What did the Lord mean by vain repetition? It includes idle and meaningless words, saying much and meaning little. Some people have the habit of talking a lot and saying little or nothing! Beware that this is not characteristic of your time of prayer. It certainly will not be so if you begin to discipline yourself in your approach to God, for although you will approach God reverently, yet as there is nobody else at hand to be impressed, you can discard meaningless forms and phrases. In the secret presence of the most High, you will discover that you too (as did God's servants of old), may speak with the Lord face to face. It is an opportunity to frankly but truly chat matters over with the One Who knows the answers to all the problems and Who is able to make all grace abound toward you, so that in all the events of the day you may abound unto every good work. Thus the life of Christ will be radiant through you, because you have been to the place and had the time and a purpose in prayer.

TELEGRAPHIC PRAYER—
ANY PLACE AND ANY TIME

" A TIME and place for prayer! Why, I thought you could pray anywhere and at any time." "Yes," says another, "and if you are going to pray in a certain place it is going to be mechanical, something like heathen worshippers who go into a temple to pray."

It is not contradictory to the previous chapter to state quite emphatically that prayer can be *at any time* and *in any place*. The previous emphasis was on forming the habit of prayer. Habits have a way of revealing themselves in unexpected ways. When the person is off-guard or suddenly thrust into an unexpected situation, that which has become a true and settled habit of life asserts itself quite naturally but nevertheless quite definitely. It is a habit! Habits are revealed by actions.

When you have formed the habit of prayer, then this will have gone a long way to making it true in your experience that prayer is an attitude of life and because it is a habit, you will be habitually turning to the Lord in prayer. This again is revealed in the life of the Lord as, for instance, in John 11: 41, where the Lord Jesus lifts up His eyes and also His heart in prayerful thanksgiving as He stands before the tomb of Lazarus. Likewise, as the Lord confronted the hungry multitude, He lifted up His heart in thankful prayer to His Father. This was the attitude of His life. It is manifested in the very situations which, to the onlooker, might have appeared critical, if not almost disastrous. In an emergency you react according to certain habits which have been formed in secret through the unseen events of life.

There is scarcely a greater example of this in the Old Testament than Nehemiah. Incidentally, Nehemiah is a man whose life and service was characterized by great activity. The Christian worker can learn much from the Book of Nehemiah. In view of his activity, it is striking and worthy of note to observe that Nehemiah was an outstanding man of prayer. First of all, as the need of God's people and the city of Jerusalem was made known to him, he at once turned to God in prayer. "And it came to pass, when I heard these words, that I sat down and wept, and mourned certain days, and fasted, and prayed before the God of heaven" (Nehemiah 1: 4). The whole of the chapter should be read if you would learn how to pray. We pass on into Nehemiah, chapter 2. In a moment of emergency which could have been one of great peril to Nehemiah, we read his first reaction to the question of Artaxerxes the king is "so I prayed to the God of heaven" (Nehemiah 2: 4).

Because Nehemiah was a man of prayer he became also a man of faith and a man of action, a man who was willing to place himself at the disposal of God—but that is rather straying from the point that we are making at the moment, which is that prayer can be *at any time* and *in any place*. In chapter 4, Nehemiah is confronted with the hostility of Sanballat and Tobiah, who mock and ridicule the work of the rebuilding of the city wall, and in such a moment Nehemiah telegraphs to the Lord, "Hear, O our God; for we are despised . . ." (Nehemiah 4: 4).

The opposition continues to increase, joined to Sanballat and Tobiah are the Arabians, the Ammonites and the Ashdodites who enter into a conspiracy to come and fight against Nehemiah and his workers. In such a moment, there is only one thing that Nehemiah can do—"Nevertheless, we made our prayer unto God, and set a watch against them day and night, because of them" (Nehemiah 4: 9).

There is unexpected misrepresentation and difficulties from within, and as Nehemiah faces this misrepresentation again he telegraphs on high: "Think upon me, my God, for good, according to all that I have done for this people" (Nehemiah 5: 19). Further opposition is met in the same way, "Now therefore, O God, strengthen my hands" (Nehemiah 6: 9). In every emergency Nehemiah reveals the habit of his life. He is a man of prayer. In similar circumstances, others would have panicked, despaired, given up the work—or even resigned! Not so Nehemiah—he knew an unfailing source of strength, a refuge in the storm, a God with whom he was in ceaseless communication.

Is it so with you? Has lack of place and time and purpose in prayer robbed you of this further privilege of ceaseless communion with the Lord? Are you going to allow it to continue to rob you of this unfailing sufficiency which Christ makes available to you?

Now we cannot but help think and turn again to the scripture "Pray without ceasing" (1 Thessalonians 5: 17).

Of course you will do this—if the habit has been formed. You will want to pray continually. You will be unceasing in prayer. You will never stop praying. You breathe without ceasing. You breathe continually. You never stop breathing whilst you live. You do not need somebody to tell you to breathe. Why, no, this is elementary—but is it true of your prayer life? From the secret place you go forth into a day that will have its difficulties, its trials, a day in which unceasing demands will be made upon you, but you are in touch with God, you have the life of Christ, you can draw upon His sufficiency, and the sweetness of the presence of the Lord will abide, for by prayer you reveal your dependence upon Him. He is your life, therefore you pray as naturally as you breathe.

PRAYING WITH THANKSGIVING

A RE you taking time to turn to the scriptures to which we are referring and quoting? It will be helpful if you do so. Have you noticed the next verse to that which we last quoted in 1 Thessalonians, chapter 5? "In every thing give thanks: for this is the will of God in Christ Jesus concerning you" (1 Thessalonians 5: 18).

Did you also notice that the two instances to which we referred in the life of the Lord revealed Him giving thanks to the Father as He faced a tremendous need? The Lord prayed without ceasing and in everything gave thanks. He knew that His Father had an answer for every situation. He knew that as His life was committed to the Father, and as He went about doing the Father's will, so God would surely undertake. Therefore, He spoke to His Father in prayer and gave thanks no matter what the circumstances were. This, we are told, is God's will for each one of us who are in Christ Jesus. Whatever happens, give thanks to God in every situation. No matter what the outward circumstances may be, if you are walking in fellowship with the Lord and doing His will, though you may not know the answer, you will know that God has an answer. In faith you may give thanks. Likewise, you may give thanks even in the trying situations, knowing that in this way God is not only blessing and developing your own Christian experience and leading you to spiritual maturity, but out of it you will be the better fitted to be used by Him in days to come. In every thing give thanks! This is the will of God in Christ Jesus for each one of His children.

As this injunction is carried out, you will at once see that you will be delivered from the use of prayer simply as a 'give me' exercise. Indeed, in fellowship and thanksgiving with the Lord you will doubtless come to know the secret of the Lord. You will discover the spontaneous fulfilment of the preceding verse, "Rejoice evermore" (1 Thessalonians 5: 16). Praying continually and giving thanks have a habit of going together. The praying and thankful Christian is also the joyful Christian.

You cannot do better than turn to Philippians 4: 6, where once again the emphasis is on praying with thanksgiving, "Be careful for nothing; but in every thing by prayer and supplication with thanksgiving let your requests be made known unto God".

But, you say, my needs are many. They are varied, they are constant—that's good! Have no anxiety about your needs. God is able to make all grace abound toward you. God is able to liberally supply your every need. Paul wrote to the Christians in Philippi, and it is still true, "But my God shall supply all your need according to his riches in glory by Christ Jesus" (Philippians 4: 19). God calls upon you to exercise faith in Him and in all circumstances and in every situation to lift up your heart in prayerful thanksgiving, making your needs known to Him, and yet at the same time thanking God in faith and anticipation of His provision. Thus you will be glad in the Lord. You will rejoice in Him. Pray with thanksgiving and you will rejoice with continual gladness.

Philippians 4: 6—Colossians 4: 2—1 Thessalonians 5: 16-18. Yes, they should be marked in your Bible and become part of the very fibre of your Christian experience.

TRUE AND EFFECTIVE PRAYER

A NOTHER question now needs to be considered and that is concerning the effectiveness of prayer. No sooner is this question raised than at once the answer is given, 'Why, yes, of course prayer is effective', but nevertheless, deep down in many hearts, is the feeling that prayer has not always been as effective as it might have been, or at any rate, something seems to be lacking. Before we go further, let us turn to one or two Scriptures in the Gospel according to John. First of all, John 14: 12-14: "Verily, verily, I say unto you, He that believeth on me, the works that I do shall he do also; and greater works than these shall he do; because I go unto my Father. And whatsoever ye shall ask in my name, that will I do, that the Father may be glorified in the Son. If ye shall ask anything in my name, I will do it."

I need hardly remind you that these words were spoken by the Lord Jesus Christ to His disciples as He was speaking of the coming of the Holy Spirit Who now dwells in the heart of every true believer. It is because the Holy Spirit has come into our hearts that the child of God can be used by the Lord to accomplish His purpose and service now—but we concern ourselves in particular with verses 13 and 14. Nevertheless, it is important to remember that these verses can be true in our experience because of the presence of the Holy Spirit within. He brings the very Life of Christ so that it is true for us to say that "because He, the Lord Jesus, lives, we live also" (John 14: 9). Furthermore, because of the presence of the Holy Spirit in our hearts, the next verse is also true—

25

"At that day ye shall know that I am in my Father, and ye in me, and I in you" (John 14: 20). Likewise, John 14: 23—"Jesus answered and said unto him, If a man love me, he will keep my words; and my Father will love him, and we will come unto him, and make our abode with him".

At new birth, the Holy Spirit brings the Life of Christ and henceforth we are in Christ and Christ is in us; His life has become our life and in experience we begin to discover the truth promised by the Lord: "At that day ye shall know that I am in my Father, and ye in me, and I in you." The Lord's prayer for His disciples in John 17 also becomes fulfilled in our experience.

> "That they all may be one; as thou, Father, art in me, and I in Thee, that they also may be one in us; that the world may believe that thou hast sent me. And the glory which thou gavest me I have given them; that they may be one, even as we are one; I in them and thou in me, that they may be made perfect in one; and that the world may know that thou hast sent me, and hast loved them, as thou hast loved me" (John 17: 21-23).

Now we return to the two statements which the Lord made. "Whatsoever ye shall ask in My Name, that will I do . . . if ye shall ask any thing in My Name, I will do it." Whatever you ask! Ask anything! Ah, yes, but there is a little qualifying phrase—"In My Name". Having considered the Scriptures concerning the coming and the implications of the Holy Spirit dwelling with the believer, we can now begin to understand something of the meaning of that little phrase "In My Name", Does it mean just tagging on at the end of your prayer a phrase, such as "for the sake of Jesus Christ" or even, more briefly still, "for Christ's sake, Amen". No, no, it is something far more wonderful than that! It is related to the life of the child of God, the new life which has been brought by the Spirit of God and is, therefore, none other than the life of Christ. It is important that you follow closely. The Lord said, 'Verily, verily' as He spoke of this truth, as if to say, "Whatever you do, do not miss this. Take special note!"

What does the Name mean? The Name refers to the Person of the Lord Jesus. The Name represents His character, indeed *all* that He *is*, so that to pray in His Name is none other than to allow the Lord Himself to express Himself through you. It is the believer that makes the request, and yet the request comes from Christ through the child of God. It is Christ thinking through the believer, it is Christ's mind becoming the mind of the believer, it is His will being done and exercised through our will. You ask whatsoever you will, but it is not really your will but Christ's will being exercised through you.

Turn to the familiar Scripture, Galatians 2: 20. The principle stated there has to become practical in every department of our life if Christ is living in us.

> "I am crucified with Christ: nevertheless I live; yet not I, but Christ liveth in me: and the life which I now live in the flesh I live by the faith of the Son of God, who loved me and gave Himself for me" (Galatians 2: 20).

Let us re-word this verse and yet, in doing so, it is not to do it an injustice in emphasizing the particular manifestation of the Life of Christ in the believer which we are considering at the moment. "I am crucified with Christ: nevertheless, I live and pray and ask whatsoever I will; yet it is not I that asks and prays but it is Christ, Who lives in me, Who is seeking and praying through me, and the prayer which I now offer in the flesh is offered through the faith of the Son of God Who lives in me and prays through me."

As we have previously stated, it is in John 14 that the Lord is teaching His disciples concerning the coming of the Holy Spirit and the implications of His coming. Then, as we read on into chapter 15, the Lord uses a very delightful, simple and yet wonderful illustration to make known further

the unity that henceforth exists between the Lord Himself
and believers. He likens Himself to the vine, the Father to
the husbandman and believers to the branches. One aspect
of the life of abiding in Christ is that it is a prayerful life
which knows the joy of answered prayer.

> "If ye abide in me, and my words abide in you, ye shall
> ask what ye will, and it shall be done unto you. Herein
> is my Father glorified, that ye bear much fruit; so shall
> ye be my disciples . . . Ye have not chosen me, but I
> have chosen you, and ordained you, that ye should go
> and bring forth fruit, and that your fruit should remain:
> that whatsoever ye shall ask of the Father in my name,
> he may give it you" (John 15: 7, 8, 16).

Here again, the tremendous potential and possibilities of
prayer are stated: "ye shall ask what ye will . . . whatsoever
ye shall ask, it shall be done unto you"! As you abide in
Christ, so the Life of the Lord is expressing itself through you.
His will has become your will; your will has been surrendered
to His will; it is part of the practical outworking of the Life
of Christ in you as much as the life of the vine is the life of
the branches. Every action of the branch is henceforth a
manifestation of the life of the vine. It is the nature of the
branch to bear the fruit of the parent vine, that is, luscious
bunches of grapes. This is in perfect keeping with the life,
activity and purpose of the vine. It would be an abnormal
vine if it did otherwise! But let us use rather an extreme,
even absurd, illustration—for sometimes the very absurdity of
an illustration will enforce the point.

Imagine for a moment that a certain branch becomes
articulate! We are also relating this illustration to the desire
of an unthinking and possibly immature Christian who, when
first reading that whatsoever he asks will be granted, demands
the handsome motor car! But now it is the branch that is
speaking and it says: "I want to bear figs". The vine replies
"No, it is my nature to enable you to bear grapes". But the

branch is insistent. "I want to bear figs; give me figs! figs! figs! I want to bear figs!" Again the vine replies: "But it is not my nature to bear figs. I want you to bear grapes, much fruit in the form of beautiful grapes". But the branch is still insistent: "It is figs I want to bear; figs or nothing else. Figs! FIGS! FIGS!" What happens? The life of the vine is thwarted. No longer does it pulsate freely through the branch, but the branch, insistent that it bears figs, begins to shrivel and becomes barren. Finally it withers and is cut off as a branch—it does not bear fruit, it will not bear fruit and it is cast from the vine because it was not the will of the vine that it should bear figs. This 'branch' is very much like some Christians!

"Ah," says somebody, "Here is the promise—whatsoever I ask, anything that I ask, God will do it." "Well, now," says one young fellow, "I want a fast sports car!" A girl says, "I want . . ."—well, what *does* a girl want? And some other person says, "It would be rather nice if we had enough money so that we did not have to bother about working any more!" Another says, "I would like a new house" and so you could multiply the requests. Things! Things! THINGS! THINGS! If you pray on these lines—maybe some of you have been doing so in a greater or lesser degree—has your prayer been effective? Has the promise been fulfilled? You shudder to admit it, but if you are honest the answer is 'No'. But does that mean something is wrong with the promise? Indeed, to probe deeper, these questions must be asked, 'Has this been true prayer, prayer in the Name? . . . or just a travesty, a twisted conception of what prayer really is? . . . nothing but a further expression of the self-life.'

But here is another branch on that same vine. As it draws upon the life of the parent vine it murmurs, "All I want to do is to experience your life flowing through me, producing wonderful, beautiful grapes; I am available—I want you to have more of me, I want you to have all of me. I want you to possess me to the full, I want you to express yourself through me; this is my will"—the life of the vine flows freely and fully and the fruit appears, much fruit, more fruit.

When this is true of you as a Christian, God is glorified and in that way you become a true disciple of the Lord Jesus. The will of the vine has become the will of the branch. The will of the vine is expressed through the activity of the branch.

Now translate this into the realm of prayer of which we are thinking in particular at the moment. As you abide in Christ and draw upon His life and sufficiency in all things, so you delight to do His will, for His will has become your will. The things that He loves, you love; the things that He wants to see accomplished, you desire to see accomplished. A new effectiveness and potentiality in prayer opens up before you, for you pray according to His will; you pray in His name and you have the petition that you ask of Him. 'It shall be done' says the Lord, for in that way the Father will be glorified in the Son.

> "And in that day ye shall ask me nothing. Verily, verily, I say unto you, Whatsoever ye shall ask the Father in my name, he will give it you. Hitherto have ye asked nothing in my name: ask, and ye shall receive, that your joy may be full" (John 16: 23 and 24).

> "And this is the confidence that we have in him, that, if we ask any thing according to his will, he heareth us: And if we know that he hear us, whatsoever we ask, we know that we have the petitions that we desired of him" (1 John 5: 14 and 15).

The same truth is clearly stated in Romans 8: 26-27:

> "Likewise the Spirit also helpeth our infirmities: for we know not what we should pray for as we ought: but the Spirit itself maketh intercession for us with groanings which cannot be uttered. And He that searcheth the hearts knoweth what is the mind of the Spirit, because he maketh intercession for the saints according to the will of God."

This is the secret of truly effective prayer—the Holy Spirit interpreting the mind of Christ to you and then leading you out in prayerful supplication and so making known your requests.   More will be said about this in the next chapter. Henceforth, there is a further reason for praying always with thanksgiving, for you are praying according to His will; your desire is His desire because His desires have become your desires.   It is the fulness of the Life of Christ within; this is the Life of the Vine flowing freely and finding expression in the branch.   This is your life, hid with Christ in God.

VII

LED BY THE SPIRIT IN PRAYER

TRUE prayer in its deeper and more profound aspects origin-
ates in and springs from God Himself. It comes from
the heart of the Father and is implanted in the heart of the
child of God by the Holy Spirit. Prayer is an expression of
the desire, of the mind and will of God. These desires are
brought by the Holy Spirit to the believer and so the desire
of heaven becomes the prayer of the Christian for that which
is in the mind and will of God has been born in the heart,
mind and will of the child of God through the ministry of the
Spirit of God. In true prayer, the child of God takes that
which the Holy Spirit has first laid upon his or her heart and
again by the Spirit, that prayer is offered through the Son
Who presents it at the Throne of Grace.

Let me repeat this again briefly, for I believe it will be
helpful to a true and fuller understanding of the power and
potentiality of prayer. True prayer emanates from the mind
and will of God and is conveyed by the Holy Spirit to the
believer, thus making real the same desires in the heart, mind
and will of the child of God. The praying is thus in accord
with the mind and will of God in heaven. The believer on
earth prays in the Spirit and so the prayer is presented by the
Son at the Throne. Briefly, we might state it thus: from the
Father, by the Spirit, to the child of God; through the Spirit,
to the Son, back to the Throne. Having thus sought to state
this simply, as 'a circle of prayer', and to summarise a glorious
truth in few words, I want to add that we must not be too
mechanical in our thinking or try to over visualise that which
is of the Spirit and which is, therefore, spiritual.

As you take time to think over these things, it will lead in many instances, to a new concept of prayer. Prayer will be seen as that which draws the child of God into a closer understanding and realisation of the will of the Father. It is by prayer that God calls the believer into co-operative fellowship and activity with Himself.

I have already used the illustration of the boat hook. Bear this in mind. Throw the hook—line, lay hold of the jetty! Pull on the line and little by little, you are brought alongside of the jetty until you are right there. Pray! Pray with persistence! Remember prayer is not our trying to change the mind and will of God until He comes into line with our petty little ideas, but one of the true and chief purposes of prayer is that little by little we are drawn more and more into line with His mind and will so that He can then implement His will through us. Allow this truth to come home to your heart and mind and prayer will assume new significance and it will also serve to emphasise that prayer is not so much our getting from God as God being given the opportunity to reveal more and more of Himself and His ways to us. It will also lead to greater joy in prayer. His joy will be flowing to us and our joy will be full and overflowing to others.

Now let us turn to a number of scriptures which bear out the truth that we have been considering. The first is found in John's Gospel and is within the section which contains the Lord's teaching concerning His forthcoming departure and the coming of the Holy Spirit, so that the Lord is speaking of prayer within that context, namely, after that the Holy Spirit has come to dwell in the heart and life of the child of God. It is as a result of the regenerating work of the Holy Spirit that the believer becomes a sharer in the life of Christ and henceforth is "a partaker of the divine nature" (2 Peter 1:4).

"And in that day ye shall ask me nothing. Verily, verily, I say unto you, Whatsoever ye shall ask the Father in my name, he will give it you. Hitherto have ye asked nothing in my name: ask, and ye shall receive, that your joy may be full" (John 16: 23-24).

In this instance then, the Lord is speaking of prayer after that the Holy Spirit has taken up residence in the believer's heart and life. It is prayer under the direction and impulse of the Spirit of God. It is effective prayer, tremendously worth while and results in fulness of joy. It is prayer in the Name of Jesus.

What does it mean "to pray in the Name of Jesus"? It does not mean that if we tag on at the end "for Christ's sake" or some such similar phrase that all will be well. It means something far more than that. The child of God is a sharer of the divine nature and to pray in His Name is to pray in perfect union with all that Jesus is and with His authority. You do not pray in His Name by merely adding "for the sake of Jesus Christ" but only as you allow the Holy Spirit to bring and interpret to you the mind of Christ. Then you pray according to His will and with His authority and you have the petition that you desired of the Lord, for, in point of fact, it is in accordance with God's mind and will.

Turn now to James 5 and the latter part of verse 16:

"The effectual fervent prayer of a righteous man availeth much" (James 5: 16b).

A righteous man is one who is rightly related to God. This new relationship comes about through receiving the Lord Jesus Christ and as a consequence of the presence of the Holy Spirit in the life. The earnest prayer of one such releases the mighty power of God. For this reason, the righteous man walking in fellowship with God, is in tune with the Almighty and prays according to His mind and will.

Another scripture already quoted but which we quote again because it speaks of the great potential of prayer is found in John's First Epistle:

"And this is the confidence that we have in him, that, if

we ask any thing according to his will, he heareth us:
And if we know that he hear us, whatsoever we ask, we
know that we have the petitions that we desired of him"
(1 John 5: 14-15).

Praying according to the mind and will of God gives
certainty and purpose in prayer and faith can say "Thank You"
in advance because of the confidence we have in Him.

Why should God choose to call us into this co-operative
activity with Himself by prayer? It is all of His grace and
by His loving kindness. God can work without us but He
has chosen to use human instruments to be partners with
Him in the accomplishing of His purposes.

One of the great chapters in the Bible on the effectiveness of
the work of the Holy Spirit in the life of the child of God is
Romans 8. This also has something to say to us on this
great theme of praying in the Spirit.

"Likewise the Spirit also helpeth our infirmities: for we
know not what we should pray for as we ought: but the
Spirit himself maketh intercession for us with groanings
which cannot be uttered. And he that searcheth the
hearts knoweth what is the mind of the Spirit, because
he maketh intercession for the saints according to the
will of God" (Romans 8: 26-27).

The Spirit intercedes in us and through us and on our
behalf in perfect harmony with the will of God. Allow the
Spirit of God to exercise this ministry of intercession through
you. Failure so to do, inevitably results in the quenching of
the Spirit and there is corresponding loss of joy and effectiveness in prayer.

The Epistle to the Ephesians speaks of the believer's iden-
tification with Christ in heavenly places. In the last chapter
of the Epistle, we read of the Christian's armour and in verse
18 we are reminded of one of the most effective weapons of
the child of God. It is the weapon of "all-prayer".

"Praying always with all prayer and supplication in the

Spirit, watching thereunto with all perseverance and supplication for all saints;" (Ephesians 6: 18).

For us, at the moment, the important phrase is "praying . . . in the Spirit". The Holy Spirit interprets the mind and will of God to the believer. The believer prays but it is "in the Spirit". It is Spirit inspired, Spirit directed, Spirit controlled. You and I are called upon by God to use this weapon of "all-prayer" but as we do so, it is not us but the Spirit in and through us. Dare we neglect to avail ourselves of such a mighty weapon, whether it be in respect of our personal life or in service for the Master?

The same truth is stated clearly and concisely in Jude's Epistle:

"But ye, beloved, building up yourselves on your most holy faith, praying in the Holy Ghost" (Jude 20).

Prayer is far deeper and more wonderful than a perfunctory few words in the morning and a hurried "Goodnight", as it were, at the end of the day. No . . . No . . . prayer is something more than that! There will be days when by reasons of various pressures and duties there will not be much opportunity for being alone with the Lord but the more we realise the true nature of prayer and rely upon the Spirit, so much more will the Spirit, unquenched and ungrieved, lead us out in prayer, even as we are engaged in other activities during the day.

In the Old Testament there is a telling illustration of prayer which reveals the significance of prayer in its more profound and deeper implications, such as those of which we have been speaking. Before, however, turning to these Old Testament references, we will consider one or two verses in the New Testament which bring out the picture which is presented to us in the Old Testament.

"And when he had taken the book, the four living creatures and four and twenty elders fell down before the Lamb, having every one of them harps, and golden vials full of

odours (or incense), which are the prayers of saints"
(Revelation 5: 8).

The marginal reading gives the word "incense" in place of
"odours". From this scripture, it will be seen that the
incense is representative of "the prayers of saints".

"And another angel came and stood at the altar, having a
golden censer; and there was given unto him much
incense, that he should offer it with the prayers of all
saints upon the golden altar which was before the throne.
And the smoke of the incense, which came with the
prayers of the saints, ascended up before God out of the
angel's hand" (Revelation 8: 3-4).

In this scripture also, there is reference to the ascending
incense as being representative of the prayers of God's people.
We will look at one other New Testament reference. Turn
back to Luke's Gospel, where it states that whilst the incense
was being offered up in the Temple, the people were engaged
in prayer in the outer courts.

"And the whole multitude of the people were praying
without at the time of incense" (Luke 1: 10).

Now we are ready to move back into the Old Testament
and we shall see that the offering up of incense was chosen
and ordained by God to be a lovely and apt picture or rep-
sentation of the prayers of God's people.

"Let my prayer be set forth before thee as incense; and
the lifting up of my hands as the evening sacrifice"
(Psalm 141: 2).

The incense was not to be made according to man's idea
and if it were, it would be counted as false incense or false
fire and would be totally unacceptable unto God. It would
be an abomination unto the Lord. The incense had to be
made according to God given instructions which the Lord
made known to Moses. You should read these directions
very carefully.

"And the Lord said unto Moses, Take unto thee sweet
spices, stacte, and onycha, and galbanum; these sweet
spices with pure frankincense: of each shall there be a
like weight: And thou shalt make it a perfume, a confec-
tion after the art of the apothecary, tempered together,
pure and holy: And thou shalt beat some of it very small,
and put of it before the testimony in the tabernacle of the
congregation, where I will meet with thee: it shall be
unto you most holy. And as for the perfume which
thou shalt make, ye shall not make to yourselves according to the composition thereof: it shall be unto thee
holy for the Lord. Whosoever shall make like unto that,
to smell thereto, shall even be cut off from his people"
(Exodus 30: 34-38).

In these words, strict instructions were given as to the
composition, that is, from which spices, the incense was to
be made. It was stipulated that this incense was to be used
for no other purpose than as an offering unto the Lord. It
was to be not only sweet and fragrant but also pure and holy.
Furthermore, it was forbidden to use it for any personal or
selfish ends—"it shall be unto you most holy . . . it shall be
unto thee holy for the Lord".

So now, the Holy Spirit reveals the mind and will of God
to us His children so that we in turn can praise, adore and
worship Him aright and offer up our supplications to the
Lord in perfect accord with God's mind and will—for His
glory and not for mean and selfish ends. It is a wonderful
and holy exercise to pray thus unto the Lord. It is inspired
by and derived from the Spirit and is well pleasing unto the
Lord.

In this same chapter in Exodus, we read these words:

"And Aaron shall burn thereon sweet incense every
morning: when he dresseth the lamps, he shall burn
incense upon it. And when Aaron lighteth the lamps at
even, he shall burn incense upon it, a perpetual incense

before the Lord throughout your generations" (Exodus 30: 7-8).

Aaron and the priests of old went into the Holy place to trim the lamps every morning and evening and at the same time they were to offer this sweet incense to the Lord—*every morning and each evening*.   Does that suggest anything to you? Does it remind you of something we have said in an earlier chapter?

There are those who say "It is not necessary to pray every morning or each evening—I pray when I most feel like it or when there is a special need".

There is, however, good scriptural ground for suggesting that it is desirable and well pleasing to the Lord to make time for regular prayer, praise, worship and adoration every morning and each evening. We have already pointed out that there is clear teaching in scripture on this point and also the example of the Lord Jesus. Moreover, I trust that now it is becoming more and more clear that praying is not just a question of asking, asking and asking—rather like presenting God with a shopping list—but enjoying your fellowship with God the Father by the Spirit through the Son and thus allowing God to make known His mind and will to you. As you enjoy this fellowship, you will pray according to the will of the Lord. You will begin to understand something of His purpose for you for that day and you will be open to His leading through the events of the day. You will be led by the Spirit and you will walk in the Spirit.

Do you say: "Nothing ever happens—I never meet anybody who is concerned with spiritual matters to whom I can talk of the Lord"? May I ask you another question? Do you pause to offer sweet incense unto the Lord and so give Him time to communicate His will and loving purposes to you? Aaron offered sweet incense every morning, each evening, it was continual and constant, "a perpetual incense before the Lord".

I want to draw your attention to an incident in scripture which fits in perfectly with the picture we have had of prayer as incense offered unto the Lord and yet also illustrates the need and place of 'telegraphic' prayers. The regular offering of incense morning and evening which as we have seen suggests regular times of prayer (choose the place and keep the appointment!) does not rule out 'telegraphic' prayer (any place and any time).

In Numbers, chapter 16, we read of judgment followed by plague falling upon the people of God because certain of their number were disobedient and presumed to worship God in their own way. In this moment of catastrophe and emergency, Moses calls upon Aaron to go forth and offer incense.

> "And Moses said unto Aaron, Take a censer, and put fire therein from off the altar, and put on incense, and go quickly unto the congregation, and make an atonement for them: for there is wrath gone out from the Lord; the plague is begun. And Aaron took as Moses commanded, and ran into the midst of the congregation; and, behold, the plague was begun among the people; and he put on incense, and made an atonement for the people. And he stood between the dead and the living; and the plague was stayed" (Numbers 16: 46-48).

Moses says to Aaron 'Go quickly'—I rather like that! This is a good illustration of telegraphic prayer in a moment of special need but it arises out of a habit and practice that has been formed every morning and each evening.

Later we shall be considering the place and practice of prayer in the life of our Lord. We can learn much from His example in praying as for instance from the following scripture:

> "And in the morning, rising up a great while before day, he went out, and departed into a solitary place, and there prayed" (Mark 1: 35).

There are other references in the Gospels which speak of

the Lord spending time alone with His Father in prayer—early in the morning and going out at eventide, even spending whole nights in prayer. He lived His life and served God in complete dependence upon His Father and enjoyed fellowship in prayer. He calls upon us to do likewise—"As my Father hath sent me, even so send I you" (John 20: 21).

Make this your prayer, "Lord, teach us to pray".

Allow the Holy Spirit to direct and lead you into the joyful experience of a full and effective prayer ministry in co-operative activity with the Lord Himself who has become your life by His indwelling Spirit. Pray in the Spirit!

VIII

DOES GOD ALWAYS ANSWER PRAYER ?

Does God always hear and answer prayer?

When the question is put as simply and as bluntly as that, most would at once reply, "Yes, of course God hears and answers prayer". But if the questioner is a little more persistent and says, "Yes, but does He *always* hear and answer prayer?", with the emphasis on 'always', what then? Always?

It would seem as if God's honour is at stake to say anything other than, "God always hears and answers prayer". Yet having said that, perhaps not always with the conviction that it might be stated, there are those who, deep down in their heart, would like to whisper in an undertone, "But I know one or two instances where there does not seem to have been any answer!"

It has been pointed out in an earlier chapter that one of the principal purposes of prayer is to bring us into closer fellowship with the Lord. It has already been stated that if we are abiding in Christ, then it will be the life of the Lord that is expressing itself through us. This will govern the desires of our heart and we shall be asking according to His will. Likewise together we have considered the scripture in Romans 8: 26-27. No doubt you will desire to re-read these verses and now your attention is further directed to the following scripture:

"And this is the confidence that we have in him, that, if we ask anything according to his will, he heareth us; And if we know that he hear us, whatsoever we ask, we

know that we have the petitions that we desired of him"
(1 John 5: 14-15).

From these scriptures and the general teaching of the Word
of God, it will be seen that the closer we are walking with
the Lord, so will our requests be made in accordance with
His will and we shall know that we have the petitions that
we desired of Him. We can, therefore, make them known
with thanksgiving, that is, in anticipation of the prayer being
heard and answered.

It may, nevertheless, be helpful to consider different ways
in which God grants the answer to the petition that we offer.
It will be helpful if we think of these answers in four ways.

First of all, there are direct answers to prayer. DIRECT
ANSWERS—there is no difficulty here. A request is made
and to the joy and delight of the child of God, an answer
comes speedily. The heart is filled to overflowing with
renewed joy and thanksgiving to the loving heavenly Father.
This would frequently seem to be the experience of a very
young Christian, and in this way, no doubt, God sees fit to
encourage the new believer or the young child. In the experience and biographies of certain of God's servants who have
been greatly used, they have sometimes testified to the fact
that in the earlier days of their Christian experience, they
found that answers to prayer came more readily than in
later years. There is a reason for this which we shall be
considering later, but nevertheless the direct answer to prayer
should be the portion of every true child of God right through
his or her life. We do, however, observe that this is sometimes found to be particularly frequent in the experience of
a young Christian.

For a scriptural example, turn to Acts, chapter 4, and as
you read of the early church praying, from verse 23 onwards,
the answer is stated to have come even as they were assembled
together—read Acts 4: 23-31. No wonder the Apostles went
out and with great power gave witness to the resurrection

of the Lord Jesus and great grace was upon them all. Like-wise, in 2 Kings 6: 17, we have the offering of prayer by Elisha and the answer immediately granted: "And Elisha prayed, and said, Lord, I pray thee, open his eyes, that he may see. And the Lord opened the eyes of the young man; and he saw; and, behold, the mountain was full of horses and chariots of fire round about Elisha." In the following verse, there is another prayer and immediate answer: "And when they came down to him, Elisha prayed unto the Lord, and said, Smite this people, I pray thee, with blindness. And he smote them with blindness according to the word of Elisha" (2 Kings 6: 13).

Here is a young teenager. He has been away on holiday to a special House Party for young people of his own age. There he has come face to face with the claims of the Lord Jesus Christ and has received Him into his heart. He returns home and is thrilled to bits with his holiday and above all with the great discovery he has made. He wants to go to another House Party during the next school holiday and as he is still recounting excitedly to his parents all that has happened while he has been away, he suddenly puts the question to Dad and asks him if he could go again at Easter. It would hardly seem an opportune moment to ask Dad to consent to a further holiday so soon after the extra holiday already granted at Christmas. The one has only just finished and yet, to the boy's delight and also in some measure to his surprise, father gives his consent. As the boy tells of the incident a short time later, he says, "I prayed and God heard and answered my prayer, for, frankly, I did not think Dad would say 'yes'." A Direct Answer to prayer.

Quite frequently there are answers to prayer which truly are answers but in a different way from that anticipated. A DIFFERENT ANSWER FROM THAT ANTICIPATED. Most Christians who have known the Lord for a little while can look back with great joy at the way in which God has answered prayer, but in a totally different way from that which they expected and invariably they have discovered that God's answer was exceeding abundantly above all that they asked or thought. God has exceeded their expectations. For instance, we discover that Paul invites the Christians in Rome to pray that he might come to them with a prosperous journey. Of this you can read in Romans 1: 10 and 15, 28-33. God certainly heard Paul's prayer and took the Apostle to Rome. You can read of this in Acts 28: 16 onwards. As one version puts it: "So we came to Rome". That journey outwardly appeared to be full of tremendous danger and trials and yet in all the changing circumstances of the journey God overruled and used these events to His glory. Paul was given the opportunity to witness before many people and particularly to persons in high places. Prayer was answered, but hardly in the way that Paul or believers in Rome originally expected. It was a Different Answer from that anticipated.

There is also the classic example connected with the conversion of Augustine. As a young man, Augustine was leading a very loose and wayward life. His godly mother, Monica, constantly prayed for him and when she heard that he was going to Italy she feared that this would only be to his further undoing. She gave herself to prayer, indeed, spending a whole night in prayer, that God would intervene and prevent her son from going. That night, Augustine sailed and duly arrived in Italy. It was there that he met Ambrose and was thus led to a personal faith in the Lord Jesus and was converted. As Augustine so aptly sums up the incident concerning his mother's prayer: "He answered not her prayer, but granted her heart's desire".

A young man due to take a service was hurrying for the bus, the only one that would get him there in time. To his dismay, before he arrived at the bus stop he saw the bus departing. He knew he was too late and had been praying that God would hold up the bus for him. Can God slow down a bus? Can He make things run late according to schedule? Why, yes, of course He can—but He does not always choose to work in that way! As the young man immediately began to step it out on the road, he thumbed a lift and very shortly a car stopped and drove him quite near to his destination, incidentally overtaking the bus en route. Therefore he arrived earlier and without payment of fare! But even more important, as he revealed the purpose of his journey to the driver of the car, it gave him the opportunity to bear testimony, not without result. It was a different answer from that which he expected, but is another instance of a Different Answer in which God exceeded the expectations of the one praying.

There are other matters which have been made the subject of prayer for a long period of time, even for years, and there appears to be a very Delayed Answer.   DELAYED ANSWERS—in this connection it is good to read Daniel chapter 10. Twice over, Daniel, the man of prayer, is spoken of most highly. "O Daniel, a man greatly beloved . . . O man greatly beloved, fear not." Yet we discover in verse 2 that Daniel was praying for three whole weeks, no doubt acknowledging the sin of his people and pleading the fulfilment of God's promises, for that is the subject of his prayer in the preceding chapter. Nevertheless, he has no assurance or peace as to the answer, but then the word is spoken to him, assuring him that he has been heard.

> "Then said he unto me, Fear not, Daniel; for from the first day that thou didst set thine heart to understand, and to chasten thyself before thy God, thy words were heard, and I am come for thy words" (Daniel 10: 12).

In the next verse it is stated that there has been opposition from one who is referred to as 'the prince of the kingdom of Persia'. This is usually interpreted as referring to one of the principalities or powers of the heavenly places and the whole incident suggests spiritual conflict being waged in heavenly places. This is not an incident that we can fully understand. Attention is drawn to it now, as it may at times have a bearing on this subject. It must not, however, be overlooked that the Lord to Whom we make known our requests is the One Who is the Victor over all.

Nevertheless there appear to be delays in the answering of prayer on certain occasions which are designed by God to develop, strengthen and lead on the child of God. For instance, it is not always good to grant a child a request immediately he or she asks. It would soon lead to lack of appreciation and true sense of values. The Apostle James has a very pertinent word in this connection, for we read in his Epistle, chapter 4 verse 3, these words:

> "Ye ask, and receive not, because ye ask amiss, that ye may consume it upon your lusts."

This verse suggests an entirely wrong motive, an asking so that when the answer is granted it may be wrongly used and not for the glory of God. We are going to come back to our original illustration of prayer being like the boat hook, to bring us into closer fellowship and alongside of God's will and purpose. A delay may be necessary so that this relationship be deepened lest an immediate answer be to the un-doing rather than the wellbeing of the one praying. Delay may also be necessary so as to develop perseverance and the habit of prayer.

In the First Book of Samuel, chapter 1, we read of Hannah the wife of Elkanah, who was childless, desiring with all her heart a child. No doubt she prayed often that this reproach of having no children might be taken from her and the desire of her heart fulfilled in the birth of a little baby. One can well imagine that if she had had a child at that point he would have been the darling of the home, the apple of his mother's eye, petted and pampered and thoroughly spoiled. God had other purposes. He desired a boy who would grow up to be a man of God, a priest and prophet of His people, one who would be a leader of His chosen people Israel.

Hannah finally reached the place where, whilst still desiring a boy with all her heart, she was willing to surrender all, the longed-for boy included, to the Lord and submit to His will.

> "And she vowed a vow, and said, O Lord of hosts, if thou wilt indeed look on the affliction of thine handmaid, and remember me, and not forget thine handmaid, but wilt give unto thine handmaid a man child, then I will give him unto the Lord all the days of his life, and there shall no razor come upon his head" (1 Samuel 1: 11).

In due time the child was born and handed back to the Lord. Thus, by reason of the delay, Hannah was brought to the point at which God could fulfil His will. She said:

> "For this child I prayed; and the Lord hath given me my petition which I asked of him; Therefore also I have lent him to the Lord; as long as he liveth he shall be lent to the Lord. And he worshipped the Lord there" (1 Samuel 1: 27-28).

Later the boy became a man of God, a priest and prophet of His people, the man God wanted him to be.

In connection with Delayed Answers there is also an instructive incident found in Matthew 15, where in verse 21 we read that Jesus "departed into the coasts of Tyre and Sidon". It was not often that He went over the borders and out of Palestine. Read for yourself the whole incident in Matthew 15: 21-28. Observe the passionate prayer of the woman of Canaan and notice the Lord's attitude at first: "He answered her not . . .". Then, when His disciples urged Him to do something, saying, "Send her away; for she crieth after us", He reminded them, "I am not sent but unto the lost sheep of the house of Israel". Was the Lord indifferent to the need of this woman? Was He indifferent to the grievous condition of her daughter? Did He not hear her cry? Was this a case of hardness of heart, of strict conformity to formality in not granting the request of one who was not of the house of Israel? Read on. Even as this woman of Canaan came and worshipped the Lord saying, "Lord, help me", He again made an answer which, to say the least, did not seem to be encouraging. He spoke in the picturesque form of speech familiar to people of the East and which was readily understood by the woman. She, with quick wit sharpened, no doubt, by her great need and the urgency with which she was now making it known, went on to make an apt rejoinder to press her need again. In verse 28 it is stated, "Then Jesus answered". Why did Jesus only answer then? It was not because He was unmindful of her need. It would seem that He had gone particularly to the coasts of Tyre and Sidon to meet such a woman in her need. Why then not an immediate answer? Here was a woman who had faith, but the Lord drew her out in such a way that her faith became great faith. She was strengthened and developed in her confidence in the Lord. If experience has taught us anything, in all probability she was filled with even greater joy and delight when the answer came than if she had obtained an immediate answer.

Here is a young lad 11 plus, nearly 12. His friends have bicycles and he begins asking Mum and Dad for a cycle of his own. It is mid-summer and the request is repeated with monotonous frequency day after day. His fond parents tell him he is too young, it is too dangerous, it is too expensive, he has other things to do. They give all the varied reasons that parents can for not giving their boy a bicycle! Summer wears away into autumn and autumn into winter and it is Christmas Day. The box-room has been kept mysteriously locked for some little time, but now the great morning has arrived and at the appointed time the key is placed in the boy's hand and he turns the key in the lock, throws open the door and there, to his delight, is a brand new bicycle. His joy knows no bounds! He hugs both Mother and Father and says, "Mum, Dad, you're simply wonderful!" Has the boy lost anything in waiting? If anything, his joy is greater now than it would have been if the request had been granted back in the summer. Have his parents lost anything by way of respect in the boy's estimation? Not at all. If anything, he respects and loves them all the more.

Now we come to a further answer—Denials. DENIALS —there are times when God sees fit to say 'No', and 'No' is just as much an answer as 'Yes'. Why should God say 'No'? Is this an answer? Let it be repeated once more that this also may be to develop His child and it is not to deny simply for the sake of denying. Possibly there are four reasons why God sees fit to say 'No'.

In the first place, it may be because God has something better in store in future days, so that this first request is not necessary in the light of what He is going to do in the future.

Then, secondly, God may see fit to say 'No' because He knows it would be unwise to grant the request. Such a request, if granted, would be ruinous to the believer's Christian character. For instance, a little baby seeing the brightly shining carving knife on the table, stretches out his hand. Does the mother or father at once grant the request? If anything, the knife is put a little further out of reach of baby hands. It would be unwise to commit a knife into the hands of one so young. The baby cries and frets and pouts. Does this make mother or father change their minds?

Think for a moment of young Christians honestly and sincerely desiring to be used of the Lord. They offer their prayer, but God says 'No'. To grant their request would be ruinous and prove to the undoing of the wellbeing of their Christian character as, for instance, when a young man prayed to the Lord that Spurgeon would allow him to preach from his pulpit at the Metropolitan Tabernacle. To grant such a request would almost certainly have led to pride and being puffed up, quite apart from the young man being totally inadequate for such an opportunity. When God did not see fit to grant the prayer, the young man went and asked Spurgeon for himself. Spurgeon also said 'No'!

The third reason why God may see fit to say 'No' is because the prayer is based on an imperfect knowledge of God's will and ways. This may be due again to spiritual immaturity or arise out of a lack of understanding of God's Word.

Finally, maybe God sees fit to say 'No' because the petitioner is not abiding in Christ and the believer's own state of heart and relationship with the Lord is such that God in His wisdom is bound to say 'No'. When Israel of old was not living in fellowship with the Lord, the Lord's power was just the same but God was prevented from doing all that He wanted to do on behalf of His people.

> "Behold, the Lord's hand is not shortened, that it cannot save; neither his ear heavy, that it cannot hear; but your iniquities have separated between you and your God, and your sins have hid his face from you, that he will not hear" (Isaiah 59: 1-2).

Prayer out of a wrong motive, offered on the basis of a desire for self-glory or self-indulgence, must receive 'No' for an answer.

> "Ye ask, and receive not, because ye ask amiss, that ye may consume it upon your lusts" (James 4: 3).

In thinking of occasions when God sees fit to say 'No', there spring to mind two outstanding examples in the New Testament when the Lord saw fit to give 'No' for an answer. In the early part of Luke, chapter 5, we read of the miraculous draught of fishes which led Simon Peter to fall down at the feet of the Lord and say, "Depart from me; for I am a sinful man, O Lord". In later years, Simon Peter must have been so thankful that the Lord gave 'No' for an answer to that prayer. The Lord remained faithful, even when Peter himself was not always as faithful as he might have been. Instead of departing from Peter, the Lord had come to save him and to dwell within him from the day of Pentecost and to be with him for ever.

Likewise, in the experience of the Apostle Paul we read of this great man of God praying three times that the troublesome thing to which he refers as 'a thorn in the flesh' might be removed from him. Was it removed? Did the Lord take it away from him so that he might no longer be hindered by it? God gave him 'No' for an answer, but read on:

> "And he said unto me, My grace is sufficient for thee; for my strength is made perfect in weakness. Most gladly therefore will I rather glory in my infirmities, that the power of Christ may rest upon me" (2 Corinthians 12: 9).

Does Paul mourn over this answer to his thrice offered prayer? No, he rejoices that God saw fit to answer this way.

> "Therefore I take pleasure in infirmities, in reproaches, in necessities, in persecutions, in distresses for Christ's sake, for when I am weak then am I strong" (2 Corinthians 12: 10).

It is said of the saintly Bishop Taylor Smith that, as a young man, when he led his first soul to Christ he got away as soon as possible—if I recall correctly that of which I have read—to a nearby, half-built and empty house and, kneeling down, prayed, "Lord, lettest now thy servant depart in peace"! But the Lord knew better than to answer that prayer with a straight 'Yes'. God said 'No' because He had larger purposes for His dear servant. Taylor Smith's later prayer was so wonderfully answered in his own experience. "Lord, if it be possible, prove the possibility of the divine in the human." Those who knew Bishop Taylor Smith recall a very true and gracious manifestation of Christ that was discernible in the Bishop's own life and character.

In this connection, there is a lovely incident in the early childhood of Amy Carmichael. The story goes that Amy observed as a little child of only three or so years old, how those with blue eyes were admired. She had two big brown eyes. Prior to going to bed one night and before saying her prayers, she turned suddenly to her mother and said, "Mummy, does Jesus always hear and answer prayer?" To which Mother said, "Why, yes, of course He does, dear" and so, with the determination of a three year old, Amy said, "Then I am going to ask the Lord Jesus to give me two blue eyes!" Kneeling, and with childlike simplicity, she asked God to give her two blue eyes by the morning. She went to bed happily—had not mother said that Jesus always hears and answers prayer? As she awoke in the morning, suddenly she remembered her prayer of the night before and, jumping out of bed, she dashed over to the dressing table and, clambering up to look in the mirror, what did she see? Two lovely blue eyes? Oh no! Soon her two brown eyes were filled with tears as she went to unburden herself to her mother. Why had Jesus not heard and answered her prayer? But Jesus had heard. He had answered. "Came a whisper soft and low; Jesus answered—He said 'No'." Years later Amy Carmichael realized God's wisdom in giving her two brown eyes for, dressed as an Indian woman, she would go undetected to the heathen temples of India to rescue the little girls who were being sold into a life of impurity.

'No' is just as much an answer as 'Yes'.

IX

THE LORD'S PATTERN PRAYER

"LORD, teach us to pray."

Thus requested the Lord's disciples as they beheld the Lord praying in a certain place. "Lord, teach us to pray!" It is more important that we should pray than know just how to pray and then omit to do so. Pray—and you will learn how to pray! You learn how to pray by praying!

In response to this request the Lord set out a model or pattern prayer. This is often called the Lord's Prayer and inasmuch as it was the Lord Who first uttered it in teaching His disciples, it is the Lord's Prayer. It might, however, be more appropriate to reserve this title for the prayer offered by the Lord and recorded in the 17th chapter of John's Gospel. It may also be helpful to think of the words that are more generally known as The Lord's Prayer as a model or pattern prayer. Better still, maybe, as The Family Prayer, for it can only be truly used by those who have become members of God's family by new birth and an acceptance of Christ.

If you read the opening verses of Luke, chapter 11, you will discover that the Lord responded to the request "Teach us to pray", by quoting the now familiar prayer. He then follows this by a parable on prayer in which prayer is related to a very practical situation in life. It cannot be over-emphasized that as we pray so we are brought into closer fellowship with God, but it is always with this purpose— that we might be the more useful to Him in the practical situations of life. Therefore, true prayer always issues in a life which glorifies God in the ordinary situations of everyday life.

You will be helped in your praying as you read the prayers that are recorded in Scripture, both in the Old and New Testaments, but for a moment or two let us survey the model or pattern prayer uttered by the Lord as He taught His disciples to pray.

It needs to be emphasized that there is no hard and fast rule regarding the form of true prayer. Words can be framed very correctly according to outward forms and yet carry little or no meaning. God looks upon the heart. Nevertheless, we should seek to order our approach to our eternal and loving heavenly Father in a right and fitting manner. This seems to be the purpose that the Lord had in mind as He taught His disciples to pray. The words of this prayer are familiar enough. Their very familiarity may mean that we have begun to over-look or completely forget their meaning. To repeat the words parrot-fashion means nothing and is certainly not praying.

The Lord said unto them, "When ye pray, say, Our Father which art in heaven". This at once declares the relationship between the petitioner and God. It is an intimate and yet reverent approach. It is the child, a member of the family, coming to the Father, yet it is the Father Who is in heaven. Therefore, it is the approach of the worshipper who comes and acknowledges that this One Whom he delights to call Father is also his God. How lovely to remind ourselves at this point of the words of the Lord Jesus, spoken to Mary Magdalene after His resurrection:

> "Jesus saith unto her, Touch me not; for I am not yet ascended to my Father; but go to my brethren, and say unto them, I ascend unto my Father and your Father; and to my God and your God" (John 20: 17).

Come to God in prayer, then, with the intimacy of a child speaking to the Father and yet also with the reverence of a worshipper approaching God.

"Hallowed be Thy Name." This is a recognition of the absolute sovereignty and supremacy of God. The Name represents the character of the Person. His Name stands for all that He is—His Sovereignty and His Holiness. He is sanctified, set apart. There is none like unto Him. There is none to be compared unto Him. He is God and there is none else. This at once reveals the spirit of worship and adoration and recognizes that the Lord is God and nothing less than the homage of the heart is fitting to be offered to such a One.

"Thy Kingdom come." To pray thus implies that the petitioner desires the coming of the kingdom and of the King. This at once relates itself to Christian service and a preparedness to meet the coming King. If I pray for the coming of the King and the kingdom, then I shall also present myself to do His bidding, to hasten His coming.

"Thy will be done, as in heaven, so in earth." You cannot truly pray this prayer without at once being challenged in your own heart as to whether you desire His will to be done in your own heart and life. Are you prepared to obey the Lord implicitly? Your will to be surrendered to His will? You cannot disobey, if these words are truly *your* prayer. This speaks, then, of the believer's obedience and readiness to do the Lord's bidding.

"Give us day by day our daily bread." Thus need and dependence are made known. It is an acknowledgement of the child's need and dependence upon God the Father, not only for the material daily bread that meets the needs of the physical body, but also for that spiritual food which sustains the child of God in the Christian life. Yet this phrase takes us a step further, for it says, 'day by day' or 'daily' which means that you are prepared to trust God to supply your need day by day. In other words, it implies a continual dependence upon God.

"And forgive us our sins; for we also forgive every one that is indebted to us." This surely speaks of the manifesting of the life of Christ in daily life, for as the child of God has received mercy, so there is the need to show mercy and a forgiving spirit. "And grieve not the Holy Spirit of God, whereby ye are sealed unto the day of redemption. Let all bitterness, and wrath, and anger, and clamour, and evil speaking, be put away from you, with all malice; And be ye kind one to another, tender-hearted, forgiving one another, even as God for Christ's sake hath forgiven you"—Ephesians 4: 30-32. This is God manifesting Himself through the child of God to others. As the Christian prays thus it is encumbent upon the petitioner to walk in the light and manifest Christ to the world.

"And lead us not into temptation, but deliver us from evil." This speaks of the committal of the life to the Lord, that the pathway may be directed for the day by God. His guidance is claimed and His deliverance is sought.

"For thine is the kingdom, and the power, and the glory, for ever. Amen." This doxology is found in Matthew 6: 13. It is a further recognition of the sovereignty, supremacy and triumph of God. It speaks of praise and of thanksgiving. God is your Father and as a member of His family you share His triumph. He is able to do—to Him is committed all power and you may count on Him.

We have looked at these words very briefly, but it will be seen that they declare and emphasize the relationship that is ours with God, leading to true worship and the presenting of our bodies for service in full and glad obedience. They then go on to declare our dependence upon God and desire that the life of Christ might be manifested through us, leading to a committal of the life day by day into the hands of God. They end with a doxology ascribing confidence in and praise to the Almighty power of an Almighty God.

As you study this prayer along these lines, it should prove helpful in ordering your own approach to God. Words can be meaningless, but they are intended to be full of meaning and truly expressive of the desires of the heart and the thoughts of the mind.

"Lord, teach us to pray."

X

PRAYER—
PRACTICAL AND PERSISTENT

Prayer is practical. Prayer should be related to the everyday events of this life. This is so beautifully illustrated by
the homely illustration that the Lord uses following His
teaching of the disciples to pray.

> "And Jesus said unto them, Which of you shall have a
> friend, and shall go unto him at midnight and say unto
> him, Friend, lend me three loaves; For a friend of mine
> in his journey is come to me, and I have nothing to set
> before him? And he from within shall answer and say,
> Trouble me not; the door is now shut, and my children
> are with me in bed; I cannot rise and give thee. I say
> unto you, Though he will not rise and give him, because
> he is his friend, yet because of his importunity he will
> rise and give him as many as he needeth" (Luke 11: 5-8).

To the Lord's first hearers, this is a situation which might
easily have arisen and with which they would be familiar.
We can easily translate it, as it were, into our own circumstances. As a matter of fact, it is only recently that a friend
travelling in the Middle East arrived rather late at a wayside
inn. After knocking loudly and repeatedly in an endeavour
to arouse the inn-keeper, he was hailed from an upper window
and in reply to his inquiry received an answer in almost
exactly the same words as used in the Parable. This was done
quite unwittingly on the part of the inn-keeper—saying that
he could not be bothered now, for the door was shut and he
and his children were in bed. In a moment we shall be

thinking over this illustration, but in the meantime we must not overlook the Lord's application:

> "And I say unto you, Ask, and it shall be given you; seek, and ye shall find; knock, and it shall be opened unto you. For every one that asketh receiveth; and he that seeketh findeth; and to him that knocketh it shall be opened" (Luke 11: 9-10).

The Lord's illustration needs no explaining—a good illustration never does. The Lord goes on rapidly to the application, following this with thought-provoking questions which further apply the truth that He has been teaching.

> "If a son shall ask bread of any of you that is a father, will he give him a stone? Or if he ask a fish, will he for a fish give him a serpent? Or if he shall ask for an egg, will he offer him a scorpion? If ye then, being evil, know how to give good gifts unto your children; how much more shall your heavenly Father give the Holy Spirit to them that ask Him?" (Luke 11: 11-12).

God is more ready to hear and answer prayer than we are to pray! He delights to give good gifts unto His children.

As we further consider this illustration, let us now seek to discover all that the Lord was teaching His disciples in answer to the original request, "Lord, teach us to pray". In the preceding chapter, we have considered the approach to God. Lest any should think that prayer is such a spiritual exercise that it is only for the quiet room, only for flights of spiritual ecstasy, or sublime moments, we find that the Lord's illustration demonstrates that in the emergencies and dilemmas that arise in the ordinary course of daily events, prayer is going to be the secret of triumph and supply the power to proceed triumphantly through every situation. In other words, prayer is practical—prayer is related to the everyday events of life!

A further outstanding point emphasized here is that prayer

is to be persistent.   If there is one truth that verse 8 teaches, it is this—persevere in prayer!   This brings us back to one of our earlier thoughts on prayer becoming a habit and a regular habit of life.   Never give up praying!

> "Praying always with all prayer and supplication in the Spirit, and watching thereunto with all perseverance and supplication for all saints" (Ephesians 6: 18).
> "Continue in prayer, and watch in the same with thanksgiving" (Colossians 4: 2).

How easily some folk give up praying and so frustrate the purposes of God in some measure as far as they are personally concerned.   They will not yield to the maturing and refining work of the Spirit of God in bringing the supplicant to that position where God can answer the prayer exceeding abundantly above all that the one praying asks or thinks. Observe the progression which is stated in verse 9: "Ask . . . seek . . . knock . . ."   From simple request to more concentrated seeking and on to continual and determined knocking.   There is a progressiveness about prayer, which as we have seen, allows God to work out His purposes in a fuller and deeper way.

How many people are referred to in the Lord's parable? There are three persons: You . . . a friend in need . . . a rich friend.   In point of fact, it is really a friend in need on life's journey . . . you in the centre . . . the rich friend who can supply the need.   *You* are the vital link between the need and the supply.   We could stop to dwell upon the significance of this story from more than one angle, but suffice it to say that God is seeking to work through you to make available His riches to many a needy and weary traveller on life's way.   But for the moment we concern ourselves with the manner of the request, that is, the prayer offered to the rich friend.

In passing, let it be noticed that the one referred to as you in the parable (is it *you* to whom the Lord is speaking?)

takes upon his own heart the need of his friend. He is filled with compassion. Although the hour is inconvenient, he sallies forth. If there is no compassion for the needs of others, there will be little or no intercessory prayer on behalf of others. Prayer that is not costly will achieve little or nothing in relation to interceding for others in their dire spiritual need.

How did the man in the parable pray? First of all, he makes a simple and direct approach. You may have thought that as we looked at the phrases of the Lord's model or pattern prayer, that these sounded a little sanctimonious, but observe now the simplicity and directness of the approach— "Friend . . . FRIEND".

> "What a Friend we have in Jesus . . .
> What a privilege to carry
> Everything to God in prayer."

As simple and direct as that. The term here used is "Friend" but it is the same approach as earlier when it was as a child to the father. Nothing could be more direct and shorn of undue ceremony.

The request is definite—"Lend me three loaves". He knew what he wanted. He knew what his friend in need wanted and he asked for it, but alas, and one says it kindly, so many prayers seem to be characterized by a strange indefiniteness, as if it is left to the Lord to sort out the blessings that are required. Of course *He* knows! . . . but it is good that we, as His children, should acquaint ourselves with the need and then be definite. If you are going to be persistent, you will need to be definite. If you are definite, it will also help you to be persistent. Know and ask accordingly.

Next there is found a confession of personal need and inability to supply that which is so sorely required by the friend who has come in from the highway. "I have nothing to set before him." What an honest statement this is—a recognition of personal bankruptcy! To translate it into other words, we might say, "Lord, here is a need to be met, which I cannot meet of myself, but You can and I lay claim that You do so by reason of my living relationship with You". Be honest in your praying. Let it be pointed out once more that here in this simple prayer there is no flowery language. Time is precious. The need is urgent.

What persistence is here revealed! The love that drove this man out into the darkness because of his needy friend keeps him knocking. He will not be put off. He cannot be put off. He cannot meet the need, but the need is there all right and there is One Who can meet the demands of the situation.

May I remind you? Your rich Friend can meet every need! Here see how faith is exercised. Likewise, as you persist in intercessory prayer, so your own faith will be exercised and developed. Difficulties and obstacles have a habit of calling out the best and developing character.

But the story does not end there. There is a rich reward. He is given "as many as he needeth". This man would have returned with a joyful heart and arms full, but I think that that joy would have increased to overflowing as he saw his needy friend tucking in and deriving all the benefit of that which he had been unable to supply himself, but which he had obtained from his wealthy friend. The needy one is satisfied, he also is satisfied—there is joy on every hand.

Do you know this joy in response to prayer, or do you easily grow cold and give up? Never cease to pray! Recognize your privilege and responsibility as one who, in God's plan and purposes, is a key to a desperate situation. Come to your loving Lord direct and with definite prayer requests, acknowledging your own need and persistently lay claim to the riches available in Christ. This you may do with confidence and therefore with thanksgiving.

"Be careful for nothing; but in every thing by prayer

and supplication with thanksgiving let your requests be made known unto God" (Philippians 4: 6).

"Continue in prayer, and watch in the same with thanksgiving" (Colossians 4: 2).

"Pray without ceasing. In everything give thanks; for this is the will of God in Christ Jesus concerning you" (1 Thessalonians 5: 17-18).

XI

BUT IF GOD KNOWS ALREADY . . . ?

SOME questions are asked seriously. Others almost suggest facetiousness. It was, nevertheless, a question asked with due thought and in sincerity, although at first almost seeming to be a little facetious. "But why need we pray? Is it necessary to do so if God knows everything, including our needs?" Then the questioner continued, "I have scriptural grounds for asking this question. For instance, read Matthew 6: 8—'. . . for your Father knoweth what things ye have need of before ye ask him'!"

It was this scripture in particular that had given rise to the question. Take time to read the preceding verses as well. These state that we Christians should not be like the heathen, who think they will be heard for their much speaking. The Lord says, "you are not to be like them"! So here is the problem. If our heavenly Father knows our needs already, why do we need to ask? In this connection there is another scripture worth thinking over. It is found in Isaiah 65: 24.

"And it shall come to pass, that before they call, I will answer; and while they are yet speaking, I will hear."

Surely this also demonstrates that God knows the need before the prayer is offered.

Does not an earthly father who already knows the needs and desires of his children frequently desire that they should make known their requests to him? It is part of the relationship between child and father. If anything, in the intimate requests made by the child, there is a deepening of that loving relationship which already exists. If the child never makes a request, it would suggest that there is some cause of estrangement between father and child.

God knows our needs! That is quite certain, but as we have already seen, one of the purposes of prayer is to bring us to the point where God can answer the request, because we ourselves become rightly adjusted to Him. Thus the petition can be granted for His glory and for our good. The Father loves to hear His children speaking to Him in trustful confidence, in simple faith, making known needs of which He is already aware. This deepens the relationship between the child of God and our Father Who is in heaven.

But bear in mind the truth stated in Matthew 6: 8. It will help to deliver you from the failing that appears to beset certain folk, who count it their duty to inform God in their prayers in such a way as if God the Father was either unconcerned or out of touch with the things relating to His children on earth! Beware of much vain repetition. In prayer you are not God's informant, you are His supplicant.

An extreme example of this is the dear man who is reported to have prayed in the prayer meeting as he was making known a certain situation, something like this: "O God, surely you would have read in the evening paper tonight that it says . . .". How often have you approached the Lord in prayer as if He did not know?

The truth stated in Isaiah 65: 24 lets in a whole flood of light upon the loving wisdom and purposes of the Lord. In this verse it says "Before they call, I will answer, and while they are yet speaking, I will hear"! Many a time it has been proved in experience that even whilst the request was being made known to the Lord, God had already taken the steps to bring about the answer. Desperate needs laid before the Lord in the form of telegraphic prayer have found an answer which was already on the way. Many of the biographies of Christian men and women testify to this truth. A need arose in far-away China, but long before that need became apparent to Hudson Taylor in China, another man of God in England had written a cheque and had despatched the letter to meet the need. Before the one called, God had moved the other to bring about the answer! This is the great and wonderful God, the loving heavenly Father, to Whom you come in prayer!

May you have this joyful experience. When it comes to pass you will not feel that the prayer was wasted effort, but rather you will be filled with new joy and wonder at the God Who is all wise, all loving and all knowing. Likewise, it will be an equal joy when you discover that you have been moved by the Holy Spirit into a certain action, only to find out at a later date that God was thus preparing the answer to the prayer of another which had yet to be offered.

How good is the God we adore! Continue in Prayer!

XII

SHOULD I STAND OR KNEEL ?

QUITE genuinely and sincerely a young Christian raises the question: "What about our attitude in prayer? By that I mean should we kneel or stand." It is a question that arises in many minds.

We have grown accustomed to kneeling in prayer on many occasions and this is usually accepted nowadays as the customary attitude of prayer. There is much to be said for it. Indeed, if and when we are praying in a place apart and alone, to do so on bended knee may be helpful in a reverent approach to the One Who is our Father and our God. It may also assist in concentrating upon the matters which will engage our attention in prayer. But even as prayer can be offered at any time and in any place, quite obviously just as truly prayer can be offered as we walk down the street, as we travel in a public vehicle. It would be an undue show and ostentatious to kneel suddenly! All believers should cultivate the habit of using precious moments in travelling and on other occasions to enjoy fellowship with their Lord. In the early days in the Old Testament, it would seem that many of God's saints prostrated themselves on the ground before the Lord. It may be that there will be occasions when, quietly and in the presence of the Lord, we shall want to do likewise. Let it be clear, however, that the stance is of lesser importance in comparison to the actual prayer. Furthermore, it must be recognized that there are those who, by reason of physical weakness and infirmity, find they are unable to kneel or to stand. There are many of God's choice servants who, because elderly, delight to sit in their chair and enjoy fellowship with the Most High.   There are others who, as invalids on beds of sickness and infirmity, have been intercessors and prayer partners in the work of the Lord.   The Lord looketh upon the heart, not upon the bodily posture.   When the heart is right with God, there will be no place for slovenliness or irreverence in the way you approach the Lord in prayer.

XIII

THE UNANSWERED PRAYER ?

U NANSWERED prayer! But surely this becomes a little contradictory. Previously, we have been considering the answers to prayer, emphasizing that God always hears and answers even if that answer is sometimes delayed or even a denial, a 'No'. All that has been said earlier on answers to prayer still stands.

Is there such a thing as unanswered prayer?

Before we answer the question, let it be said that you need to be ready for this, for the knife is going to go deep. There is one telling phrase in James 4: 2 which goes right to the heart:

"Ye have not because ye ask not."

If there is such a thing as unanswered prayer, then it is because that prayer is never offered.

Is your life prayerless? Then your unoffered prayers are unanswered prayers. Is your prayer life deathly dull, cold and formal? Then you yourself are robbing yourself of the joy of seeing God's hand at work, for He delights to hear and answer prayer, but "ye have not because ye ask not".

Let this sentence search you. Sit quietly and think for a moment. When did you last experience an overweight of joy because of the gracious way in which God answered a special request that you made known to Him? Or do you have to confess that you have not because you asked not?

Is your relationship with your heavenly Father so distant and estranged that you can seldom find time to speak to Him intimately and privately?

Do you not know where to begin?

Learn from the disciples and make their request your request: "Lord, teach us to pray."

The Lord took time and trouble to teach the little company of men who were His first disciples. They saw Him praying and wanted to pray themselves. The same Lord Jesus will take time and trouble to teach you to pray if you are willing to be taught, if you are willing to learn and proceed in fellowship with Him.

It is important that you should face this issue quietly and definitely. If necessary, face the issue on your knees and in a place apart, alone with the Lord, before proceeding further.

You can hardly expect to be instructed further and led on in your prayer fellowship with the Lord unless you are ready to pray and continue in prayer. In the following chapters we shall be considering various instances of prayer. Firstly, in the lives of two or three of the outstanding men of God in the Old Testament. Then we shall consider instances of prayer in the life of our Lord. This will be followed by a chapter on the place of prayer in the early church as recorded in the Acts of the Apostles and, finally, we shall be looking at prayer in relation to the life and service of the Apostle Paul.

XIV

OLD TESTAMENT SAINTS AT PRAYER

THERE are outstanding examples of men of prayer to be found in the Old Testament and it will be profitable to take a brief look at one or two instances in the lives of these men of old whom God was able to use so mightily.

We have previously stated that prayer is intended by God to be more than 'a one-way exercise'. Rather, is it to be 'two-way'. God speaking to man as well as man speaking to God. This is beautifully shown in Genesis, chapter 18, where the Lord says:

> "And the Lord said, Shall I hide from Abraham that thing which I do" (Genesis 18: 17).
> "And the Lord went his way, as soon as he had left communing with Abraham" (Genesis 18: 33).

Allow God to share with *you* some of His loving purpose and plans! As we read on in this chapter in Genesis, we read of Abraham's intercession and as we come to know more of God's holiness and so realise more of the sin and need of men, we too will find that there are times when we can do nothing else but fall on our face before the Lord and intercede for others.

Think also for a moment or two of Daniel. He is another outstanding man of prayer. He and his companions are in captivity and are faced with a difficult situation. What is their immediate reaction? They react in the emergency according to the habits they have formed in private.

"Then Daniel went to his house, and made the thing known
to Hananiah, Mishael, and Azariah, his companions:
that they would desire mercies of the God of heaven
concerning this secret" (Daniel 2: 17-18).

I imagine the four men getting down on their knees together
and laying the whole matter before the Lord in prayer. Did
not the Lord know already of their predicament? Why, yes,
the Lord knew, yet He still desires us to come before Him in
prayer to make known our requests. In the very act of
prayer, we declare our need and weakness and, at the same
time, our faith in and dependence upon God and give God the
opportunity to make known to us His will and purpose in the
matter.

Another striking instance of prayer in the life of Daniel is
found in The Book of Daniel chapter 6. The enemies of this
servant and saint of the Lord have conceived a plan to trap
Daniel and the decree goes forth that none is to be worshipped
save Darius the king. The Bible is a thrilling book! Do not
deny yourself the joy of reading this story in Daniel 6! The
plot is laid. The King Darius is flattered and deceived as to
the true intention of his advisers and he signs the decree. Is
Daniel going to walk into the trap that has been laid for him?
Not at all, but with calm confidence in God, he continues to
do as he always has done.

"Wherefore king Darius signed the writing and the decree."
"Now when Daniel knew that the writing was signed, he
went into his house; and his windows being open in his
chamber toward Jerusalem, he kneeled upon his knees
three times a day, and prayed, and gave thanks before his
God as he did aforetime" (Daniel 6: 9-10).

He had formed the habit of regular prayer. Amidst the
pressing duties of state and other business, Daniel is no
stranger to 'the practice of prayer'. This is one of the secrets
of his strength and true discernment. No wonder God could
trust and use him in such a high position of state in the affairs

of the empire. But God wants to be able to trust and use us also just where we are called to work and witness and serve Him. God wants to make known His will and purposes and impart to us also true spiritual wisdom and discernment. Are we going to allow God to do this? The answer will depend to a large extent on how far we are going to be men and women of prayer.

Once more in the ninth chapter of Daniel, we are presented with another outstanding feature of Daniel's prayer life as he intercedes for Israel. Such chapters and prayers as these which are recorded in the scriptures for our instruction, will amply repay time and thought given to them in study—and preferably, study on your knees before the Lord. Well might we lift up our own heart to the Lord and say, "Lord, teach us to pray as these Thy servants of old prayed and prevailed."

Another true man of prayer of whom we read in the Old Testament is Nehemiah. It is from his life that we have several outstanding instances of 'telegraphic prayer'. The Book of Nehemiah tells us of his great achievements as God's servant. Nehemiah is a man of great faith; he is a man of action and tremendous energy but a careful study of his life reveals the fact that first and foremost he was a man of prayer. His faith and actions to a very large extent sprung out of his praying. When news is brought to Nehemiah telling of the ruined state of the city of Jerusalem, how the walls are broken down and the gates burned with fire, his immediate reaction is to cast himself down before the Lord in prayer.

"And it came to pass, when I heard these words, that I sat down and wept, and mourned certain days, and fasted, and prayed before the God of heaven" (Nehemiah 1: 4).

Chapter 1 contains Nehemiah's prayer of confession on behalf of the people of God and at once he identifies himself with the sin of the people and after confession, he pleads the promises of God. This is praying! Nehemiah, like Daniel also, prayed according to God's will as revealed through His

Word. This is praying! Now you and I as New Testament believers, have both God's Word and also the Holy Spirit dwelling within to direct us in our praying so that as we pray according to God's will, we have the petition that we ask of God. This is praying!

In every situation and emergency that arises, in the face of each new difficulty and increasing opposition, Nehemiah at once turns to God in prayer. The Lord is his refuge, his strong tower, his rock and his salvation—to whom else should or could he turn? Nehemiah reacts in these various situations according to the settled pattern of his life. Habit asserts itself in the face of crisis and temptation—whether it be before King Artaxerxes as in 1: 4 or later in the face of mounting opposition. The Book of Nehemiah abounds in instances of 'telegraphic prayer', that is, prayer offered on the spur of the moment, often amidst the dust and grime of active service—but it all springs out of a heart that has long since learnt the secret of trust and communion with a God of infinite love, compassion and mercy. Things happen because Nehemiah prays! The way of service opens, difficulties are overcome, opposition is defeated, faint hearts find new strength and courage *because Nehemiah prays*. The God given task is accomplished, the wall is rebuilt and the work finished, *because Nehemiah prays*.

> "Then the king said unto me, For what doest thou make request? So I prayed to the God of heaven" (Nehemiah 2: 4).
> "Hear, O our God; for we are despised: and turn their reproach upon their own head, and give them for a prey in the land of captivity" (Nehemiah 4: 4).
> "Nevertheless we made our prayer unto our God, and set a watch against them day and night, because of them" (Nehemiah 4: 9).
> "Think upon me, my God, for good, according to all that I have done for this people" (Nehemiah 5: 19).

". . . Now therefore, O God, strengthen my hands" (Nehemiah 6: 9).

"My God, think thou upon Tobiah and Sanballat according to these their works . . ." (Nehemiah 6: 14).

"Remember me, O my God, concerning this, . . ." (Nehemiah 13: 14).

"Remember me, O my God, concerning this also, and spare me according to the greatness of thy mercy" (Nehemiah 13: 22).

"Remember them, O my God, because they have defiled the priesthood . . ." (Nehemiah 13: 29).

"Remember me, O my God, for good" (Nehemiah 13: 31).

For the moment, we must content ourselves with the examples of these three, Abraham, Daniel and Nehemiah, from the Old Testament, but surely sufficient has been said to lead us to make this our prayer—

"Lord teach us to pray, like these Thy servants of old, at all times and in every situation."

XV

THE LORD TEACHES US TO PRAY—
IN SERVICE

"And it came to pass, that, as the Lord was praying in a certain place, when he ceased, one of his disciples said unto him, Lord, teach us to pray . . ."   (Luke 11: 1).

IT is evident that the Lord Jesus made a regular habit of praying and it will be helpful if we consider briefly certain of the occasions on which it is stated that the Lord prayed. As we learn something of the place of prayer in the life and ministry of our Lord, so we shall be taught to pray and also be led to see the necessity of maintaining the attitude of prayer at all times and in all places.

In the Scripture already referred to above in Luke 11: 1, it says that the Lord was praying in a certain place. In Mark 1: 35 we read:

> "And in the morning, rising up a great while before day, he went out, and departed into a solitary place, and there prayed."

These two scriptures emphasize the point made in one of the opening chapters, namely, that prayer needs a time and a place, even as the Lord Himself taught in Matthew 6: 6. The fact that the Lord had to go out on to the hillside because He had no bedroom of His own, no quiet place in a house, will be a tremendous encouragement to many young Christians who do not have their own bedroom or who find themselves in such places where they have to share a bedroom with one or more other persons. The Lord found a way to overcome the difficulty. Likewise, where there is a real desire to meet with God, there will be a way over the practical problem which is sometimes present when you do not have your own bedroom.

There are those who are seeking to be busy in the Lord's service but find little time for prayer and quietly waiting upon the Lord. Which is the most important—prayer or so-called service? As we look at the example of the Lord Jesus, there can only be one answer to the question.

> "Now when all the people were baptized, it came to pass, that Jesus also being baptized, and praying, the heaven was opened, And the Holy Ghost descended in a bodily shape like a dove upon him, and a voice came from heaven, which said, Thou art my beloved Son; in thee I am well pleased" (Luke 3: 21-22).

The Lord Jesus was praying and the heaven was opened. The latter phrase is significant. Heaven is always open to the man of prayer. It was at this point that the Lord entered into His public ministry and the Holy Ghost descended upon Him in a new way, anointing Him for service. Thus, it will be seen from this scripture that the Lord who went about doing good and who was later to be so fully engaged in doing the will of His Father, enters into this service in the spirit of prayer and with the fulness and anointing of the Spirit upon Him.

Prayer precedes service!

There is a similar emphasis to be found in the attitude of the Apostles as recorded for us in Acts 6: 4—"But we will give ourselves continually to prayer, and to the ministry of the Word". Notice the Apostolic order: prayer first, then secondly the ministry of the Word.

Without hesitation, let it be said once again—prayer precedes service!

We have already referred to Mark 1: 35, where we are told the Lord rose up a great while before day and departing to a solitary place, there prayed. In Mark's Gospel this reference is quoted in the early days of the ministry of the Lord. It is also significant that it is found in the first chapter of the Gospel which goes on to emphasize the ceaseless activity of the Lord Jesus. Later, this activity is summed up in one telling phrase: "They had no leisure so much as to eat" (Mark 6: 31). The Lord precedes the activity of the day with prayer. Prayer prepares you for the day!

Now turn to another scripture:

"But so much the more went there a fame abroad of him; and great multitudes came together to hear, and to be healed by him of their infirmities. And he withdrew himself into the wilderness, and prayed" (Luke 5: 15-16).

In the midst of the ceaseless activity to which the Lord was called, we find that nevertheless He withdraws Himself and waits upon His Father. His strength is renewed in the heat and burden of the day. Likewise, we discover that following the feeding of the 5,000, after He had sent the multitude away, "He departed into a mountain to pray" (Mark 6: 46). In striking contrast to this incident, in Mark, chapter 9, we have the father of the afflicted boy coming to the Lord after He has descended from the Mount of Transfiguration and He says: "I spake to thy disciples that they should cast him out, and they could not." Later, the Lord gives a telling answer in response to the question put by His disciples as to why they were powerless. The Lord said unto them: "This kind can come forth by nothing but by prayer and fasting" (Mark 9: 9-29).

If you turn to John's Gospel, chapter 11, there you will read how the Lord lifted up His eyes and spoke to His Father, with thanksgiving, as He stood before the tomb of Lazarus.

Prayer empowers in the midst of service!

From these and other instances it will be seen that whilst the Lord made a time and a place for prayer, yet no situation and no amount of activity prevented Him from also being in unbroken prayer fellowship with His Father.

As related to Christian service from the example of our Lord, we re-state with emphasis:

Prayer precedes service.

Prayer prepares for the day.

Prayer empowers in the midst of service.

> "He giveth power to the faint; and to them that have no might he increaseth strength. Even the youths shall faint and be weary, and the young men shall utterly fall. But they that wait upon the Lord shall renew their strength; they shall mount up with wings as eagles; they shall run and not be weary; and they shall walk and not faint" (Isaiah 40: 29-31).

Wait upon the Lord! That you might do whatever the Lord requires of you!

XVI

THE LORD TEACHES US TO PRAY—
IN EVERY SITUATION

WE now proceed to look at further instances of prayer in the life of the Lord Jesus. You will notice from these that as the Lord faced important decisions, so there is again the emphasis on His prayerful attitude of dependence upon His Father.

"And it came to pass in those days, that he went out into a mountain to pray, and continued all night in prayer to God. And when it was day, he called unto him his disciples; and of them he chose twelve, whom also he named apostles" (Luke 6: 12-13).

This passage tells how the Lord chose His twelve apostles. He called them and separated them from among men first of all to be with Him, so that later they might be sent forth to the special service which was to lead to the constitution of the Church, following the coming of the Holy Spirit at Pentecost. But note this: the Lord considered it necessary to spend the whole night in prayer to God. In this way the Lord reveals His dependence upon the Father, even as He taught:

"Then answered Jesus and said unto them, Verily, verily, I say unto you, The Son can do nothing of Himself, but what he seeth the Father do; for what things soever he doeth, these also doeth the Son likewise. For the Father loveth the Son, and sheweth him all things that himself doeth; and he will shew him greater works than these, that ye may marvel" (John 5: 19-20).

"I can of mine own self do nothing; as I hear, I judge; and my judgment is just; because I seek not mine own will, but the will of the Father which hath sent me" (John 5: 30).

In striking contrast is an Old Testament incident, of which you may read in Joshua, chapter 9 and which is summed up:

". . . and they asked not counsel at the mouth of the Lord . . ." (Joshua 9: 14).

Prayer is necessary in times of decision. Prayer clarifies the mind, so that you are enabled to exercise true judgment according to the will of God. In this outward way there is a deepening of the inward dependence upon and fellowship with the Lord.

The Lord was called to face more temptations than those brought to Him by the devil in the wilderness during the forty days following His baptism. There was the occasion when those who had received food at His hand wished to take Him by force and proclaim Him King, thinking that He was just the One to meet their material need and also to bring about deliverance from the power of Rome. How did the Lord meet this new temptation, which would have diverted Him from His Father's will and the great purpose for which He came into the world?

"When Jesus therefore perceived that they would come and take him by force, to make him a king, he departed again into a mountain himself alone" (John 6: 15).

Thus the Lord keeps in fellowship with His Father and in line with the will of God. Likewise, it will be so in the experience of the child of God. Often there will be temptations to be faced in many different forms. These will seek to divert the believer from God's plan for his or her life. This is a particularly subtle temptation which comes to Christian workers, especially when there is a measure of blessing attending their service. The devil seeks to cause despondency when nothing appears to happen, but equally he is quick to try and overthrow by popularity and the praise and attentions of men, when there is every indication of real blessing. These subtle temptations can be overcome as prayerfully you look to the Father and so keep close to the Lord.

Prayer keeps you in accord with God's plans and purposes.

Later, the Lord is seen more particularly facing the Cross with all its attendant trials and agony. He discloses this in some measure to His disciples, but as you read, you will observe it was immediately following a time when He had been alone praying.

> "And it came to pass, as he was alone praying, his disciples were with him; and he asked them saying, Whom say the people that I am? . . . And he straitly charged them and commanded them to tell no man that thing, Saying, The Son of man must suffer many things, and be rejected of the elders and chief priests and scribes, and be slain, and be raised the third day" (Luke 9: 18, 21, 22).

One of the secrets of facing the trying situations of this life and facing them triumphantly is to be found in waiting upon the Lord in prayer and being renewed in strength for the ordeals ahead.

Quickly following on this incident, you will read that the Lord took Peter and John and James and went up into a mountain to pray:

> "And as he prayed, the fashion of his countenance was altered, and his raiment was white and glistering" (Luke 9: 29).

As the Lord prayed, so He was transfigured before His disciples. Likewise will it be with the believer today. Prayer leading to closer fellowship with the Lord Himself leads on to a great manifestation of the life and glory of Christ through the human life.

Prayer enables you to face the trials of life.   Prayer leads to the transformed life.

Reference has been made in a previous chapter to the Lord's prayerful attitude as He stands before the tomb of Lazarus. This teaches us that in the midst of Christian ministry and service we should continue to pray with thanksgiving. It is particularly applicable as we think of Lazarus being typical of those who have gone far into sin. In Christian service and ministry, we seek to bring to them the Gospel and so make known the way of salvation, but also we should claim the victory and expect God to work, for this is what the Lord did on this occasion. By prayer, He claims the victory, face to face with the work of the devil.

By prayer claim the victory which is already ours in Christ and give thanks for what God is about to do.

Let us recapitulate!

Prayer clarifies the mind in times of Decision. Prayer keeps you in accord with God's Plan and Purposes. Prayer enables you to face the Trials of Life. Prayer leads to the Transformed Life. Prayer claims Victory over the Adversary and all his Works.

XVII

THE LORD TEACHES US TO PRAY—
AS HIGH PRIEST AND ON THE CROSS

THERE are several other outstanding instances of prayer in the life of the Lord which demand careful thought. For instance, in John's Gospel, chapter 17, the Lord as our great High Priest is there interceding for us. In this prayer, His heart is laid bare as He holds holy converse with the Father, but as He prays, so He makes known His will for believers, thus throwing a wealth of light on certain aspects of the Christian life. Take time to read the chapter through carefully, observing the principal petitions that the Lord offers. Ask yourself how far these are being fulfilled in your own life for, as the Lord states implicitly, this prayer is not only for the first disciples but for all believers of all ages. There may be no real comparison between this prayer and our own experience, for this is the intercession of the High Priest. Nevertheless, every true Christian is made a priest unto our God. Ours, therefore, is the privilege to intercede on behalf of others and to lead in praising, magnifying and glorifying the Lord with our lips as well as through our life. Intercession on behalf of others is an important part of Christian service. Do you regularly pray for others—or always and only for yourself?

As the Lord nears the final agony of the Cross, we discover Him in the Garden of Gethsemane, kneeling down and praying to His Father, saying:

"Father, if thou be willing, remove this cup from me; nevertheless not my will, but thine, be done. And

84

there appeared an angel unto him from heaven, strengthening him. And being in an agony he prayed more earnestly; and his sweat was as it were great drops of blood falling down to the ground. And when he rose up from prayer and was come to His disciples, he found them sleeping for sorrow, And said unto them, Why sleep ye? rise and pray, lest ye enter into temptation" (Luke 22: 42-46).

Contrasting attitudes are revealed here. On the one hand there is the Master facing the agony of the Cross, steadfastly following the will of God and seeking to be strengthened as He faces the great issues before Him. On the other hand, there are His disciples sleeping. The Master prays! The disciples sleep! Such an instance speaks for itself—it is not necessary to press the obvious implication. Do you sleep when you should pray?

Possibly the most telling of all the occasions on which the Lord prayed is when He was enduring the agony of the Cross. First, He prays:

"Father, forgive them; for they know not what they do" (Luke 32: 34).

The Lord is fulfilling His own teaching:

"But I say unto you, Love your enemies, bless them that curse you, do good to them that hate you, and pray for them which despitefully use you, and persecute you . . ." (Matthew 5: 44).

Few things will cripple the prayer life as much as a harsh, unforgiving spirit, even if it is against those who have done you the greatest wrong.

Prayer is the secret of a forgiving spirit.

To consider these further prayer cries of our Lord from the Cross is, as it were, to stand in the Holiest of Holies. From the Cross, again the Lord lifts up His voice in an agonizing cry as He undertakes the atoning work which He alone could accomplish.

> "And about the ninth hour Jesus cried with a loud voice, saying, Eli, Eli, lama sabachthani? that is to say, My God, my God, why hast thou forsaken me?" (Matthew 27: 46).

In this instance we observe that He refers to the Father as 'my God', to be followed by the Lord's cry of confident committal of Himself into the hands of His Father:

> "And when Jesus had cried with a loud voice, he said, Father, into thy hands I commend my spirit; and having said thus, he gave up the ghost" (Luke 23: 46).

As we survey these and other instances of prayer in the life of the Lord, well might we say as did the disciples of old:

"LORD, TEACH US TO PRAY"

May we summarize once again? We are retracing our steps back through the three chapters dealing with Prayer in the life of the Lord Jesus. From these instances we learn:

PRAYER PRECEDES SERVICE

PRAYER PREPARES FOR THE DAY

PRAYER EMPOWERS IN THE MIDST OF SERVICE

PRAYER CLARIFIES THE MIND IN TIMES OF DECISION

PRAYER KEEPS YOU IN ACCORD WITH GOD'S PLAN AND
    PURPOSES

PRAYER ENABLES YOU TO FACE THE TRIALS OF LIFE

PRAYER LEADS TO THE TRANSFORMED LIFE

PRAYER CLAIMS THE VICTORY OVER THE ADVERSARY AND ALL
    HIS WORKS

PRAYER IS THE SECRET OF THE FORGIVING SPIRIT

PRAYER LEADS TO FULL CONFIDENCE IN AND TOTAL COMMITTAL
    TO CHRIST.

XVIII

THE PLACE OF PRAYER IN THE EARLY CHURCH

THE Book of the Acts records the birth of the New Testament church. It speaks of the church and of individual believers going forth as witnesses of the risen and living Lord Jesus. It is a book of action. We find also, however, that the early believers were much given to prayer. There are twenty or so references either to individuals or to groups joining together in prayer in the Acts. The first disciples were certainly men of action, but equally so they were also men of prayer. They prayed and they went into action under the impulse of the Spirit. They were men of action because they were men of prayer. Because they were men of prayer, they were men of spirit guided action. They were men filled by the Spirit of God and therefore men whose witness, service and preaching was in the manifest power of the Holy Spirit. It was effective because they were led by the Spirit in prayer and in consequent and subsequent action.

This could not be said of the disciples as presented to us in the Gospels. We have only to recall two outstanding instances to prove this. When the Lord was on the mountain top and was transfigured before the three apostles, Peter, John and James, the remainder were in the valley powerless and impotent in the face of a great need. To them the Lord said when they questioned Him as to the reason for their powerlessness:

"And when he was come into the house, his disciples asked him privately, Why could not we cast him out? And he said unto them, This kind can come forth by nothing, but by prayer and fasting" (Mark 9: 28-29).

The other instance which at once comes to mind illustrating

the lack of prayer on the part of the disciples, is when the Lord was in the Garden of Gethsemane. To the three who had been with Him on the Mount of Transfiguration, He said,

> "Watch ye and pray, lest ye enter into temptation. The spirit truly is ready, but the flesh is weak" (Mark 14: 38).

It is a different story in the Acts. The Holy Spirit has come and they are new men in Christ and as the Master prayed, so also they have become men of prayer. Furthermore, they teach and lead the early church to be a church of prayer. The gatherings for prayer in those early days would not have been the least attended of all gatherings as is so often the case with church services today. The church of the New Testament days was a praying church and a powerful church in its witness and impact upon the world. The church today in so many places is a prayerless church—and a woefully powerless church making no impact whatsoever upon the world. Are these facts related? Do they find a counterpart in your personal life? Prayerlessness and powerlessness often go hand in hand.

We shall not be able to look at every reference to prayer in the Acts but only at a chosen few.

> "These all continued with one accord in prayer and supplication . . ." (Acts 1: 14).

Men and women were one in their waiting upon the Lord in prayer in anticipation of the Lord's fulfilment of His promise. There was no strife and no division. We read on in chapter 2:

> "And when the day of Pentecost was fully come, they were all with one accord in one place" (Acts 2: 1).

It does not say specifically in this verse that they were praying but that is certainly the inference from the phrase "they were all with one accord in one place". In this setting the Holy Spirit came in fulness and power. Whilst we recognise that now every child of God is indwelt by the Holy Spirit, yet it may be worth asking the question as to why the Holy Spirit, Who is now present in the true church and in the hearts of believers, cannot work in all His mighty power? Is it because there is such a general lack of prayer? There are churches who never have a prayer meeting. There are believers who neglect the privilege and potential of private prayer. These things ought not to be! For them, the Spirit of God is quenched and grieved.

With the conversion of a great multitude on the day of Pentecost, there is no sudden dispensing with prayer now that the whole city of Jerusalem has been stirred. Following the coming of the Holy Spirit, there was great joy. They were days of gladness and ecstacy—but equally, they were days of much prayer.

> "And they continued stedfastly in the apostles' doctrine and fellowship, and in breaking of bread, and in prayers" (Acts 2: 42).

Following untold blessing and undeniable evidence of the work of God the Holy Spirit in converting many, the early Church did not dispense with prayer! They continued in prayer. As they prayed together, so also they gave thanks to God. They praised and worshipped their wonderful God and Saviour.

> "And they, continuing daily with one accord in the temple, and breaking bread from house to house, did eat their meat with gladness and singleness of heart, Praising God, and having favour with all the people. And the Lord added to the church daily such as should be saved." (Acts 2: 46-47).

Praying, Praising and true spiritual Progress have a habit of going together.

In chapter 4 of Acts, we read how the church is beginning to face rising persecution. This new and threatening situation is met on their knees.

"And being let go, they went to their own company, and
reported all that the chief priests and elders had said unto
them.   And when they heard that, they lifted up their
voice to God . . ." (Acts 4: 23-24).

The prayer that follows is one of the greatest prayers of the
Bible.   It is one you should read and re-read.   We are not
going to consider it in detail but suffice it to say, that we
cannot do better than did these early believers and disciples.
They faced opposition in prayer.   In face of mounting difficulties and threats, they focussed their attention upon the Lord
God and the Eternal Throne.   The difficulties were as great
as ever—but seen in relation to God and in the light of the
Throne of God, they became very small and the disciples went
forward with great power and great grace and witnessed with
boldness.   Prayer changes things!

In the tenth chapter of Acts, we read of Cornelius, a god-
fearing man who evidently desired to know the truth.   God is
able to communicate His will to Cornelius because he made
time to pray.   So, likewise God gives directions and guidance
to Peter to go as His ambassador as and when Peter makes
time to pray—and this at mid-day of all times to pray!

"On the morrow, as they went on their journey, and drew
nigh unto the city, Peter went up upon the housetop to
pray about the sixth hour" (Acts 10: 9).

From the example of the Lord, we saw how He would
withdraw Himself to commune with His Father in prayer, even
when pressed by the thronging crowds and here is Peter
redeeming the time in prayer whilst lunch is being prepared!
What spiritual renewal and strength we must forfeit by lack of
prayer even in the midst of the activities of the day.   This
story in Acts 10, illustrates the point we have made earlier
that it is frequently when we are at prayer that God can
reveal His will to us.   I wonder how many secrets the Lord
has wanted to share with us and we have been too busy to
stop and listen?

This same truth is to be found in chapter 13, for it is when the church and its leaders and teachers were waiting upon the Lord that the Holy Spirit made known His will and sent forth Barnabas and Saul, to be later known as Paul.

> "As they ministered to the Lord, and fasted, the Holy Ghost said, Separate me Barnabas and Saul for the work whereunto I have called them. And when they had fasted and prayed, and laid their hands on them, they sent them away" (Acts 13: 2-3).

A praying church will very soon be missionary minded. So also it will be with the individual who has given himself or herself to prayer. A praying church or a praying individual will very soon have vision from the Lord as the tremendous needs of the harvest field. It cannot be otherwise for the great Lord of the harvest is still filled with compassion for the lost, and believers in close touch with the Lord must inevitably share His compassion and burden for the lost.

> "Pray ye therefore the Lord of the harvest, that he will send forth labourers into his harvest" (Matthew 9: 38).

Praying to the Lord of the Harvest will result in a quickened realisation of the needs of lost humanity whether near at hand or to the ends of the earth but continue to pray and you cannot remain a 'visionary'. True prayer leads to action so that there will also be a sense of mission resulting in being truly missionary minded. It is inevitable and it will lead to continued prayer, to going, to giving and to discovering the mind and will of the Lord for the Church or the individual in particular. Praying in the Spirit and therefore in fellowship with the risen Lord leads to discovery of the part either the Church or the individual can fulfil in the carrying out of the great commission to go into all the world and make disciples of all nations.

For the teaching given by the Apostles to the early church on the place of prayer, we turn to the Epistles. As we might well anticipate, the exhortations to engage in true prayer are

numerous.   Consider the following selections.   It will be seen
that frequently thanksgiving and praise are linked with the
call to prayer.

> "Not slothful in business; fervent in spirit; serving the
> Lord; Rejoicing in hope; patient in tribulation; continuing
> instant in prayer" (Romans 12: 11-12).

> "Be careful for nothing; but in every thing by prayer and
> supplication with thanksgiving let your requests be made
> known unto God" (Philippians 4: 6).

> "Continue in prayer, and watch in the same with thanks-
> giving" (Colossians 4: 2).

> "Pray without ceasing.   In every thing give thanks: for
> this is the will of God in Christ Jesus concerning you"
> (1 Thessalonians 5: 17-18).

> "I will therefore that men pray everywhere, lifting up holy
> hands, without wrath and doubting" (1 Timothy 2: 8).

> "By him therefore let us offer the sacrifice of praise to
> God continually, that is, the fruit of our lips giving
> thanks to his name" (Hebrews 13: 15).

> ". . . pray for one another, that ye may be healed.   The
> effectual fervent prayer of a righteous man availeth much"
> (James 5: 16).

> "But the end of all things is at hand: be ye therefore sober,
> and watch unto prayer" (1 Peter 4: 7).

> "And this is the confidence that we have in him, that, if
> we ask anything according to his will, he heareth us: And
> if we know that he hear us, whatsoever we ask, we know
> that we have the petitions that we desired of him" (1 John
> 5: 14-15).

I want you to think carefully over the above scriptures.
Why not pause and take time to go back and re-read them?
The example and teaching of our Lord, the example of the
first believers and the teaching of the Epistles all emphasise
the necessity of engaging in prayer.   Many are prepared to
make time to learn how to preach but how few take time to

learn to pray by praying. It has been pointed out earlier in this book that it is not recorded in the Gospels that our Lord gave detailed instructions to His disciples on preaching but we do discover that he gave them teaching on praying and several of His parables were directed to this purpose, "that men ought always to pray and not faint". This, surely, indicates the importance of true prayer.

Why is it then that prayer is so often neglected in personal and Church life? Can it be that it is because for so many, prayer has become formal, almost ineffective and consequently, there is little real joy and power such as God desires us to enjoy in and through prayer? There is the need first of personal prayer and then also of praying together with other believers. There is joy to be found in both private and corporate prayer. Frequently, it is a double joy to be praying, interceding and giving thanks with other spiritually minded believers.

As we consider these scriptures from the Acts and the Epistles can we . . . dare we, say anything other than, "Lord teach us to pray"?

XIX

PAUL AS A MAN OF PRAYER

THE life of the Apostle Paul can be profitably studied from several different aspects, but one of the most helpful and challenging studies will be to observe the place of prayer in the life of this much used man of God.

It is noteworthy that when the Lord speaks to Ananias to go to Saul of Tarsus (as he then was) following Saul's arrival in Damascus, the Lord says of him:

"Behold, he prayeth" (Acts 9: 11).

Saul as a Pharisee and a Hebrew of the Hebrews had often said his prayers, but something startling and wonderful had taken place in his heart and life as a result of his encounter with the Lord on the road to Damascus. Now he was a converted man and the mark of his conversion was 'Behold, he prayeth'. It is so easy to say prayers and not to pray reminding us of the little couplet:

"I often say my prayers, but do I ever pray?"

In this connection there comes to mind a notice exhibited in a shop window selling Bibles, hymn books and prayer books. Some were bound in hard stiff covers and others in limp morocco leather. Variously priced tickets were exhibited on the respective goods and all unwittingly there was one which read, 'Limp Prayers 10/6d.'.

There was nothing limp about the prayers of the great apostle! It was a mark of his conversion. It was a mark of his Christian life and service. Several times over, Paul, under the direction of the Spirit of God, calls upon believers

to be 'followers of me' as, for instance, in 1 Corinthians
4: 16 and 11: 1, Philippians 3: 17 and 4: 9, 1 Thessalonians
1: 6, 2 Thessalonians 3: 7-9.

In the Book of the Acts, Paul the Apostle is shown to be
a man of tireless activity, but there also, reference to his
praying is to be found.   As he speaks to the Jewish mob from
the steps of the Castle in Jerusalem—Acts 22—he refers back
to an incident which had happened years previously, when
God made known His will to him, namely, that he was in
particular sent to minister to the Gentiles.   "Even while I
prayed in the temple . . . the Lord said unto me, Depart; for
I will send thee far hence unto the Gentiles" (Acts 22: 17, 21).
As Paul prayed, so God made known His will to him.   In view
of the several occasions in the Book of the Acts in which we
read that the Lord spoke to Paul, giving him either a fresh
revelation of Himself or special directions and encouragement,
one cannot help believing that it must have been as Paul was
engaged in prayer that the Lord Himself drew near in such a
precious way.   At any rate, the truth remains that as you
pray, so God is able to reveal more and more of His will to
you.

Then again, as Paul takes his farewell of the Ephesian
elders we read: "And when he had thus spoken, he kneeled
down and prayed with them all" (Acts 20: 36).

"He prayed with them all."   This was true throughout all
his ministry, as is revealed by his Epistles.   A quick glance
through the Letters of the Apostle reveals much of the prayer-
life of this tireless servant of the Lord.   He was as ardent and
as passionate in his praying as he was in his service.   He
served the Lord acceptably because he prayed continually.
He prayed continually because of the exacting demands made
upon him in his service for the Lord.   Paul is an outstanding
example of the fulness of the life of Christ being manifest in
the earthen vessel.   Therefore, his life is also a life of prayer,
that is, of dependence upon God, even as his Master lived in
prayerful fellowship with the Father.   It must inevitably be so

if the life of the Lord is being lived out through us in the power of an ungrieved and unquenched Holy Spirit. The logical sequence of Christ enthroned in the heart, will be a life of prayer.

Does this find fulfilment in your Christian experience?

A further notable feature of the prayer-life of the Apostle is that it is marked with thanksgiving as well as request. Now we turn to the Epistle to the Romans:

> "First, I thank my God through Jesus Christ for you all, that your faith is spoken of throughout the whole world. For God is my witness, whom I serve with my spirit in the gospel of his Son, that without ceasing I make mention of you always in my prayers; Making request, if by any means now at length I might have a prosperous journey by the will of God to come unto you" (Romans 1: 8-10).

These verses are all the more remarkable as, when Paul wrote them, he had not as yet visited the Christians in Rome. Here we find reference to his praying without ceasing; always in prayer for those who, to a large extent, were unknown to him, although some of his friends had already made their way to Rome, as is revealed by the greetings he sends in chapter 16. So often we cannot even find time to pray for the people we have met, let alone believers whom we have not seen face to face in other places who are standing fast for the Lord amidst much trial and opposition.

One of Paul's great prayer burdens is revealed in a later chapter of the same Epistle. It is for his brethren according to the flesh—Israel.

> "Brethren, my heart's desire and prayer to God for Israel is, that they might be saved" (Romans 10: 1).
> "I say the truth in Christ, I lie not, my conscience also bearing me witness in the Holy Ghost, That I have great heaviness and continual sorrow in my heart. For

I could wish that myself were accursed from Christ for my brethren, my kinsmen according to the flesh" (Romans 9: 1-3).

The compassion of his Master finds expression in the heaviness and continual sorrow in Paul's heart, because of the rejection by his brethren of the good news concerning the coming of Christ to be their Saviour.

How faithful are you in praying for unconverted kith and kin? For those who are nearest to you by ties of flesh and blood, but who as yet have not accepted Christ. We might even think, too, of a slightly wider circle—how often and truly do you pray for those who know not the Lord, those with whom you have contact in the ordinary business of daily life?

Proceeding to Paul's Letter to the Corinthians, we discover that although he is later to minister severe rebukes to them, many of whom are carnal Christians, yet he finds cause for which to thank God on their behalf.

> "I thank my God always on your behalf, for the grace of God which is given you by Jesus Christ; That in every thing ye are enriched by him, in all utterance, and in all knowledge; Even as the testimony of Christ was confirmed in you" (1 Corinthians 1: 4-6).

Maybe one of the secrets of the effectiveness of his rebuke was that he prayed for these Corinthian Christians and found cause to give thanks on their behalf in the presence of the Lord. Later, he makes it clear that in proof of his ministry as a minister of God, he is engaged 'in watchings and fastings':

> "We then, as workers together with him . . . in all things approving ourselves as the ministers of God, in much patience, in afflictions, in necessities, in distresses, In stripes, in imprisonments, in tumults, in labours, in watchings, in fastings; By pureness, by knowledge, by longsuffering, by kindness, by the Holy Ghost, by love

unfeigned, By the word of truth, by the power of God . . ." (2 Corinthians 6: 1-7).

Should it fall to your lot to have to rebuke other believers who are falling short of their high calling or are wayward in their Christian life and witness, first pray to the Lord concerning them and later speak in love as the Lord makes it clear that you should do so.

To the believers in Galatia, Paul also has to write a word of rebuke. This is because of their waywardness and swift departure from the simplicity of the Gospel as it is in Christ. He is writing to those whom he has led to the Lord, for whom he once interceded when as yet they were still in heathen darkness. Now he again bows in prayer that they might go on to full spiritual maturity.

"My little children, of whom I travail in birth again until Christ be formed in you" (Galatians 4: 19).

Was the Apostle's prayer-life the secret of his effectiveness as an evangelist? Was his prayer-life one of the governing factors that made him so usable in the hand of God to bring others to the Saviour?

But Paul, as a man of prayer, was never satisfied to know that people were saved. He laboured on, longing that they might also be established in the faith, filled with the fulness of Christ and in turn be used by God to manifest the life of the Lord Jesus in their mortal bodies.

XX

THE DEPTH AND SCOPE OF PAUL'S PRAYERS

WE now turn to Paul's Letter to the Ephesians. This Epistle was probably written not only to Christians in Ephesus but to those in the region round about, then known as the Roman Province of Asia. You will recall that Paul laboured in Ephesus for a considerable time. Possibly during that period, he also journeyed into the surrounding districts. Certainly as a result of the effectiveness of his ministry in Ephesus and the particular signs accompanying the fulness of the Spirit coming upon certain believers there, they went forth to places where even the Apostle himself had not gone. The whole area was evangelised. Hence the concern of Demetrius and others, of which you can read in Acts 19: 22-29.

It was a particularly fruitful time of ministry. There was a great awakening and to these Christians who had been born again by the Spirit of God out of gross heathen darkness, the Apostle writes of the mighty power that is available in Christ and of the new position of all who put their trust in Him.

First of all, however, he rejoices in the work of grace in their hearts.

> "Wherefore I also, after I heard of your faith in the Lord Jesus, and love unto all the saints, cease not to give thanks for you, making mention of you in my prayers . . ." (Ephesians 1: 15-16).

Something of the content of his ceaseless prayers for these believers is contained in the next verses:

"That the God of our Lord Jesus Christ, the Father of glory, may give unto you the spirit of wisdom and revelation in the knowledge of him; The eyes of your understanding being enlightened; that ye may know what is the hope of his calling, and what the riches of the glory of his inheritance in the saints, And what is the exceeding greatness of his power to us-ward who believe, according to the working of his mighty power, Which he wrought in Christ, when he raised him from the dead and set him at his own right hand in the heavenly places" (Ephesians 1: 17-20).

Later, in the same Letter, we find the Apostle again bowing his knees in fervent supplication for these believers:

"For this cause I bow my knees unto the Father of our Lord Jesus Christ, Of whom the whole family in heaven and earth is named, That he would grant you, according to the riches of his glory, to be strengthened with might by his Spirit in the inner man; That Christ may dwell in your hearts by faith; that ye, being rooted and grounded in love, may be able to comprehend with all saints what is the breadth, and length, and depth, and height; And to know the love of Christ, which passeth knowledge, that ye might be filled with all the fulness of God. Now unto him that is able to do exceeding abundantly above all that we ask or think, according to the power that worketh in us, Unto him be glory in the church by Christ Jesus throughout all ages, world without end. Amen" (Ephesians 3: 14-21).

Both of these passages reveal something of the depth and intensity of the Apostle's prayer-life. He rejoices that these to whom he is writing know Christ as Saviour, but goes on to pray that they might grow in spiritual stature and that they might have spiritual understanding and an increasing knowledge of God. They knew the Lord—otherwise they would not have eternal life—but Paul wanted that knowledge to grow and grow. He wanted the believers to go on and on with the Lord. In his second prayer for them in the Epistle, his heart's desire is that they might be strengthened with might by the Spirit of God in the inner man . . . that they might experience as never before in their own life the divine might and power that raised again Christ from the dead . . . that they might not in any way fall short of God's best for their life . . . that they might be filled with all the fulness of God! Prayer such as this is not the prayer of a passing minute!

Because Paul prayed, he is well fitted and chosen by the Spirit of God to write to others.

> "Praying always with all prayer and supplication in the Spirit, and watching thereunto with all perseverance and supplication for all saints" (Ephesians 6: 18).

Do you pray for others in this way?

If there was any one group of believers whom the Apostle loved above others, it was the believers at Philippi. To them he wrote his letter which was so full of joy although it was penned in a Roman prison. He rejoices in Christ—he calls upon the believers in Philippi to rejoice in the Lord and as he reflects upon his ministry there he does so with thanksgiving and in prayer for the continuance of the work of God in the midst:

> "I thank my God upon every remembrance of you, Always in every prayer of mine for you all making request with joy, For your fellowship in the gospel from the first day until now" (Philippians 1: 3-5).

> "For God is my record, how greatly I long after you all in the bowels of Jesus Christ. And this I pray, that your love may abound yet more and more in knowledge and in all judgment; That ye may approve things that are excellent; that ye may be sincere and without offence till the day of Christ" (Philippians 1: 8-11).

Having first recorded his thanksgiving and joy, as he prays for these fervent believers, his heart then goes out for them that they may abound yet more and more in knowledge and in sound spiritual judgment . . . so that they might order their conduct accordingly and thus live lives that are not only blameless but also fruitful and which bring glory to the Name of the Lord Jesus.   Once again, observe the depth and scope of such praying.   Truly, this is praying!

Paul's earthly circumstances are not to be envied at this particular time and yet because he accepts these as from the Lord and knows that God has His own rich purposes, the Spirit can use him to call upon others not to be over-anxious but in every situation and in all things to pray with thanksgiving.

> "Be careful for nothing; but in every thing by prayer and supplication with thanksgiving let your requests be made known unto God" (Philippians 4: 6).

Now we pass on to The Epistle to the Colossians.   Here again Paul is writing to believers, the majority of whom he has not met in person—Colossians 2: 1—but that does not stop him praying for them or, indeed, from giving thanks on their behalf.

> "We give thanks to God and the Father of our Lord Jesus Christ, praying always for you, Since we heard of your faith in Christ Jesus, and of the love which ye have to all the saints" (Colossians 1: 3-4).

His prayer on their behalf merges with praise and a declaration of all that Christ has done on their behalf:

> "For this cause we also, since the day we heard it, do not cease to pray for you, and to desire that ye might be filled with the knowledge of his will in all wisdom and spiritual understanding; That ye might walk worthy of the Lord unto all pleasing, being fruitful in every good work, and increasing in the knowledge of God; Strengthened with

all might, according to his glorious power, unto all patience and longsuffering with joyfulness; Giving thanks unto the Father, which hath made us meet to be partakers of the inheritance of the saints in light" (Colossians 1: 9-12).

His prayer and desire is that they might be filled with the knowledge of the will of God, so that they too might grow in spiritual wisdom and understanding . . . that this might result in a life that is worthy of the Lord . . . being well pleasing to Him and fruitful in the manifestation of the Life of Christ in all that they do . . . this in turn leading to an increasing knowledge of God . . . issuing in true spiritual strength and might . . . that they might be enabled to stand fast with patience and meet longsuffering with joyfulness . . . so that the whole life is one of thanksgiving to the Father.

Again let it be said that prayer of this depth and scope is not the prayer of a passing moment.

Paul makes this clear, for in the next chapter he states that he prays for them always with agony, labouring and working, so that there is an expenditure of energy which, he says, is nothing less than Christ Jesus working in him and through him on their behalf. This is true intercession! This is true prayer!

Because Paul prayed thus, the Spirit of God could use him and cause him to write:

"Continue in prayer, and watch in the same with thanksgiving" (Colossians 4: 2).

Probably the first Epistle that the Apostle wrote was to the Thessalonians. He sent the First Epistle to the Thessalonians shortly after his ministry there, of which you can read in Acts 17. Paul and Silas had to leave the city because of the opposition that had been stirred up by the Jews following their preaching. He left behind believers who would have to face persecution and trials for Christ's sake. He recognizes that these Christians are young in faith, that they have not had a great opportunity of coming to know the Word of God fully, but he remembers them with thanksgiving and looks forward to the time when he can be back in their midst to teach them further. So great is his desire that, night and day, he prays for the fulfilment of this longing.

> "We give thanks to God always for you all, making mention of you in our prayers; Remembering without ceasing your work of faith, and labour of love, and patience of hope in our Lord Jesus Christ, in the sight of God and our Father" (1 Thessalonians 1: 2-3).

> "For what thanks can we render to God again for you, for all the joy wherewith we joy for your sakes before our God; Night and day praying exceedingly that we might see your face and might perfect that which is lacking in your faith? Now God himself and our Father, and our Lord Jesus Christ, direct our way unto you. And the Lord make you to increase and abound in love one toward another, and toward all men, even as we do toward you; To the end he may stablish your hearts unblameable in holiness before God, even our Father, at the coming of our Lord Jesus Christ, with all his saints" (1 Thessalonians 3: 9-13).

Here is a man who is praying exceedingly that he might be able to impart that which is lacking in their faith, so that as a result they may increase in love toward one another and be found unblameable, living holy lives in anticipation of the coming again of the Lord Jesus.

Because Paul thus rejoices and prays night and day, the Spirit of God can use him in yet a further way, so that he is the chosen instrument to write:

> "Rejoice evermore. Pray without ceasing. In every thing give thanks; for this is the will of God in Christ Jesus concerning you. Quench not the Spirit" (1 Thessalonians 5: 16-19).

"And the very God of peace sanctify you wholly; and I pray God your whole spirit and soul and body be preserved blameless unto the coming of our Lord Jesus Christ" (1 Thessalonians 5: 23).

It would seem that before the Apostle had opportunity to return to Thessalonica, God was already answering his prayer. The believers there were being established and growing in the faith, although as yet the Apostle had been unable to return to minister unto them. So as he sends his Second Letter to the Thessalonians, we discover that he has further cause for thanksgiving:

"We are bound to thank God always for you, brethren, as it is meet, because that your faith groweth exceedingly, and the charity of every one of you all toward each other aboundeth; so that we ourselves glory in you in the churches of God for your patience and faith in all your persecutions and tribulations that ye endure" (2 Thessalonians 1: 3-4).

It is not always possible to go places. It is not always possible to send letters of encouragement, although this can be done much more frequently than it usually is, but you can pray and pray without ceasing and pray with thanksgiving, knowing that God is already at work answering and meeting the needs of others.

How much sleep did the Apostle Paul lose by reason of his prayers?

We find as he writes to Timothy he again speaks of praying night and day:

"I thank God, whom I serve from my forefathers with pure conscience, that without ceasing I have remembrance of thee in my prayers night and day" (2 Timothy 1: 3).

How much did Timothy owe to the prayers of Paul? Who can say? How many others are you encouraging and helping in their Christian service by praying for them regularly and repeatedly by name? Many Pastors and Evangelists know what it is to be discouraged and have to face a multitude of difficulties. Do you pray regularly for your Pastor and for other Pastors and Evangelists that you know personally? Can they count upon your prayers for them?

In this brief survey of some of the outstanding references by the Apostle to prayer, it will be seen that here is a man who is praying according to the will of God and therefore he has the petitions that he asks. He is led by the Spirit. It is the Spirit Himself Who is making intercession through him. With Paul, prayer is not the occasional thing. It is the habit of his life. It is the attitude of his life. It is a manifestation of the life of Christ through His servant.

God can use the man or woman, the young person, who learns the secret of true prayer and who *prays*.

XXI

PAUL TEACHES OTHERS TO PRAY

A NOTHER important aspect of Paul's ministry is to be seen in the fact that not only was he himself a man of prayer and prayed for spiritual maturity in the lives of others, but again and again he seeks to lead young Christians to pray, so that they in turn become men and women of prayer. This was part of his work of leading believers to spiritual maturity. In the course of doing this he also reveals how greatly he values the prayers of God's children for his own ministry. Indeed, he counts upon their prayers.

This is an evident token of his recognition of the oneness of all believers. To pray for others and to invite others to pray for you is evidence of the unity of the body of Christ. Every member of the human body is interested, so to speak, in the activities of the complete or whole body. So in the Church of Jesus Christ we are His body and members in particular. Therefore it is right that we should pray for others and we should seek to encourage others to pray— and to pray so that our own Christian life and service may be deepened and glorifying to God.

Turn back again now to The Epistle to the Romans. There you read that the man who strives in prayer calls upon others to strive also.

"Now I beseech you, brethren, for the Lord Jesus Christ's sake, and for the love of the Spirit, that ye strive together with me in your prayers to God for me; That I may be delivered from them that do not believe in Judaea; and

> that my service which I have for Jerusalem may be
> accepted of the saints; That I may come unto you with
> joy by the will of God, and may with you be refreshed"
> (Romans 15: 30-32).

Paul and the believers in Rome are sundered far apart, yet
together they can meet at the Throne of Grace. As they
pray and the prayer is answered, so they themselves will be
refreshed and renewed in spiritual things. It is a joyful
experience for them.

The Apostle recalls to the Christians in Corinth certain
of the experiences that befell him and his fellow workers in
Asia, experiences that caused them to despair even of their
life, yet for which he thanked and praised God because these
experiences led them not to trust in themselves but in God.
He recognises, however, that the prayers of the Corinthian
Christians have been part of the means used by God to bring
about these deliverances.

> "For we would not, brethren, have you ignorant of our
> trouble which came to us in Asia, that we were pressed
> out of measure, above strength, insomuch that we
> despaired even of life: But we had the sentence of death
> in ourselves, that we should not trust in ourselves, but in
> God which raiseth the dead; Who delivered us from so
> great a death, and doth deliver; in whom we trust that he
> will yet deliver us; Ye also helping together by prayer for
> us, that for the gift bestowed upon us by the means of
> many persons thanks may be given by many on our
> behalf" (2 Corinthians 1: 8-11).

Who are you helping at this present time by your prayers
for them? There are many on the far-flung mission field who
daily have to face trying situations. Their needs are many.
Can they count upon your prayers?

After having written to the Ephesian Christians of the place
of prayer in the spiritual armour of the child of God, Paul
calls upon them to continue in prayer on his behalf.

"And for me, that utterance may be given unto me, that I may open my mouth boldly, to make known the mystery of the gospel, For which I am an ambassador in bonds; that therein I may speak boldly, as I ought to speak" (Ephesians 6: 19-20).

Pray for all saints. Pray particularly for one or two who are known to you personally who have the privilege and responsibility of public ministry, or of teaching the word of God in some way or another. Pray for them, that they may speak boldly, clearly and truly, according to the Word of God. It is better to pray for a preacher than to criticise his sermon. It is better to pray for a fellow worker than to talk derogatively concerning him behind his back. Was there a more effective, a more fruitful and truer preacher of the Gospel than Paul? Yet he says, "Pray for me, that utterance may be given unto me". In this way he brings others into co-operative fellowship with him in the service of Christ.

The believers at Philippi sent more than once to supply his need in material things. They must also have been constant in prayer for the Apostle. He acknowledges that God's overruling in the things that have happened to him are proving to his own spiritual development and are as a result of their prayers. Paul could count upon their faithful praying.

"For I know that this shall turn to my salvation through your prayer, and the supply of the Spirit of Jesus Christ" (Philippians 1: 19).

God is overruling the bonds and imprisonment and by the adequacy of the Spirit is meeting his need and flowing through him in blessing to others. He has been through the mill as far as earthly circumstances are concerned. Few, if any, could have suffered more or faced more fearful trials than did the Apostle. Therefore the Spirit of God can use him to urge the Philippians to face every situation in the spirit of prayer.

> "Be careful for nothing; but in every thing by prayer and supplication with thanksgiving let your requests be made known unto God.   And the peace of God, which passeth all understanding, shall keep your hearts and minds through Christ Jesus" (Philippians 4: 6-7).

To pray with thanksgiving is to have the peace of God garrisoning your heart and mind.   Though all the world should fall about you, though all the world should array itself against you, you can thank God, for He abides faithful. He cannot fail. He will not forsake His own.   You can thank Him in every situation.

Paul follows his very practical exhortations (in Colossians 3) to the Colossian Christians with the further exhortation to continue in prayer and in particular to pray that he may be given utterance and speak boldly and effectively for Christ.

> "Continue in prayer, and watch in the same with thanksgiving; Withal praying also for us, that God would open unto us a door of utterance, to speak the mystery of Christ, for which I am also in bonds; That I may make it manifest, as I ought to speak" (Colossians 4: 2-4).

It has been pointed out already, but let it be emphasised again and again, the Apostle called upon others to pray for him in his public ministry.   Then likewise we should pray for servants of God who are called to preach and teach.   If God gives to us the privilege of speaking on His behalf, then we also should seek to bring others into co-operative prayer fellowship, that we may speak as we ought to speak, telling forth the glorious tidings of the Gospel of the grace of God in the power and demonstration of the Spirit, because others are praying.

Reference has already been made to the exhortation in the fifth chapter of The First Epistle to the Thessalonians: "Rejoice evermore; pray without ceasing; in everything give thanks . . .". And then, once again, the Apostle comes down to this short but pungent request:

"Brethren, pray for us" (1 Thessalonians 5: 25).

In the two Epistles to Timothy, there is much wise counsel for the would-be Christian worker. Therefore, you will not be surprised to discover that there is the exhortation to pray and to lead others out in the spirit of prayer, in the First Epistle to Timothy. Turn to and read 1 Timothy 2, 1 to 3 and also verse 8.

Where ever there are believers, there should be those lifting up holy hands and being instant in prayer. As surely as you, as a Christian worker, encourage others to read God's Word, so also should believers, particularly young Christians, be encouraged to pray—and to pray for others.

Another letter comes from the prison in Rome. Will Paul be released? Will he be able to return once again to the places of previous ministry? Will he be able to revisit and bring encouragement to believers who are standing fast for Christ in the cities which threw him out because he dared to proclaim the good news of a full and free salvation through faith in Christ Jesus? Does it depend upon the effectiveness of the prayers of others from the manward and human point of view? It almost seems as if it does. In that delightful personal Letter to Philemon, we read:

> "But withal prepare me also a lodging; for I trust that through your prayers I shall be given unto you" (Philemon 22).

Paul is in prison. Philemon prays. Obstacles are removed by the Hand that holds the universe. Would those obstacles have been removed if the one had not prayed? The answer may be 'yes'. But the person who prays is the one who shares in the reward and who finds great joy in knowing that in this way he or she has been called into co-operative fellowship and service with God Himself. This is the privilege of every child of God. This is the privilege of being a co-worker together with the Lord by prayer as well as in other ways.

Shall we then pray? The answer must be obvious. We need to pray. It reveals our dependence upon and our faith in God. It enables us to walk in full enjoyment of our fellowship with the Lord and come to know something of the secrets of the Lord in our own personal experiences as well as in our Christian service and witness.

Shall we continue in prayer? The Bible teaches that we should do so. The Old Testament saints were men of prayer. The Lord Jesus Christ, although the Son of God manifest in the flesh, made it His habit and took time even out of the most intensive periods of ministry to be alone with God in prayer. The Church of the New Testament preached Christ, witnessed for Christ, but above all it advanced on its knees and overcame every opposition and obstacle by prevailing prayer. The Apostle Paul was a man of prayer, although also a man of boundless energy, of unceasing activity such as the like of which I suppose there has never been any other, but prayer was one of his priorities. In his Epistles, he made no secret of the fact that he prayed for those to whom he wrote. Furthermore, he encouraged others to pray, for he realised and knew how much he owed to the prayers of other believers.

Can we do less? We can not do more! Pray! Encourage others to pray! As the Lord teaches you to pray so you will want to teach others also to pray.

Pray without ceasing. Never stop! Never give up praying! At the same time you will rejoice yet more and more in a wonderful prayer answering God and Saviour, for as you pray you will praise and so in everything you will give thanks for this is the will of God in Christ Jesus concerning you.